For Christian Lovers Only

Leader's Guide

©2009 Clarence Walker and Ja'Ola Walker. All rights reserved. Unauthorized duplication is prohibited by law.

Published and distributed by UMI (Urban Ministries, Inc.) P.O. Box 436987, Chicago, IL 60643-6987
Printed in the USA

UMI MISSION STATEMENT
We are called of God to create, produce, and distribute quality Christian education products; to deliver exemplary customer service; and to provide quality Christian educational services, which will empower God's people, especially within the Black community, to evangelize, disciple, and equip people for serving Christ, His kingdom, and Church.

For Christian Lovers Only Leader's Guide

Published by UMI (Urban Ministries, Inc.), P.O. Box 436987, Chicago, IL 60643-6987.

Founder and Chairman: Melvin E. Banks Sr., Litt.D.
President and CEO: C. Jeffrey Wright J.D.
Writers: Clarence Walker Jr., Ph.D. and Ja'Ola Walker, D.D.
Vice President of Editorial: Cheryl P. Clemetson, Ph.D.
Product Manager: Trudi Gentry
Editor: Crystal McDowell
Graphic Designer: Gargoyle Creative Services & Design

Scripture quotations marked (AMP) are taken from the Amplified Bible, Copyright ©1954, 1958, 1962, 1964, 1965, 1987 by The Lockman Foundation. Used by permission. (www.Lockman.org)

Scripture quotations marked (NIV) are taken from the Holy Bible, NEW INTERNATIONAL VERSION®. Copyright ©1973, 1978, 1984 International Bible Society. All rights reserved throughout the world. Used by permission of International Bible Society.

Scripture quotations marked (NCV) are taken from the New Century Version®. Copyright ©2005 by Thomas Nelson, Inc. Used by permission. All rights reserved.

Scripture quotations marked (NKJV) are taken from the New King James Version. Copyright ©1982 by Thomas Nelson, Inc. Used by permission. All rights reserved.

Scripture quotations marked (NLT) are taken from the Holy Bible, New Living Translation, Copyright ©1996, 2004. Used by permission of Tyndale House Publishers, Inc., Wheaton, Illinois 60189. All rights reserved.

Scripture quotations marked (GNT) are taken from the Good News Translation - Second Edition, Copyright ©1992 by American Bible Society. Used by Permission.

Scripture quotations marked (KJV) are taken from the King James Version.

Welcome to the *For Christian Lovers Only* Marriage Curriculum! You have all you need to enrich and encourage married couples of all ages and backgrounds in your ministry. The course is as easy as ABC.

Part A is the take off point of the course with a fun-filled, yet deeply meaningful retreat to reconnect couples with each other.

Part B is the crash course on communication that gives couples the tools necessary to effectively share with each other through the five dimensions of communication.

Part C is a year-long accountability training for couples to continue their lifelong journey of spiritual, emotional, and physical intimacy as they face the challenges and temptations of resisting the flesh, the world, and the devil.

The tools from the *For Christian Lovers Only* Marriage Kit may be used in a variety of settings including Sunday School, Bible School classes, marriage conferences, or on an individual basis as devotional materials for couples who desire a stronger marriage.

The *For Christian Lovers Only* Marriage Kit includes:
- Leader's Guide for weekly, monthly, and retreat sessions plus planning tools to begin a marriage ministry campaign.
- DVD featuring session intros, vignettes, and retreat teaching sessions.
- Participants Workbook
- Resource CD including Powerpoint® presentation templates and reproducible promotional materials (certificate, poster, bulletin insert, and workbook order form).

WHY YOUR MINISTRY NEEDS THIS CURRICULUM:

FACT: Christian married couples are divorcing as quickly as unbelievers.

FACT: Marriage is on the decline as more couples are cohabitating together.

FACT: African Americans lead in divorces and single parent homes.

FACT: A greater number of African American married couples are living apart compared to other races.

FACT: African-American couples have the desire for marriage enrichment courses but are least likely to have it offered in their ministries.

FACT: The church is built on families which depend on the strength of committed couples.

FACT: This curriculum saves time and money and provides a place for continued study and accountability.

Beginning with the fragmenting of the family during slavery, poverty, and a lack of education, certain negative trends have been passed from one generation to the next. As a result, African American marriages are:

1. Broken up because of extramarital affairs 65% of the time
2. More likely to lack skills of communication and negotiation
3. Less likely to have marriage enrichment programs available to them
4. More subject to the economic challenges of unemployment
5. More impacted by things that can put stress on a marriage

{ *United States. U.S. Department of Health and Human Services. Marriage, Divorce, Childbirth, and Living Arrangements among African-Americans or Black Populations. 2000. Accessed Sept. 2008. <http://www.acf.hhs.gov/healthymarriage/about/aami_marriage_statistics.htm>* }

[TABLE OF CONTENTS]

About the Authors.. 7
The ABC's of *For Christian Lovers Only*.. 9
Straight Talk to the Brothers.. 10
Straight Talk to the Sisters... 11

Part A—FCLO Weekend Retreat

The Seven P's of Retreat Planning .... 12 - 13
The Riches of a Retreat.. 15
FCLO Retreat Schedule.. 16 - 17
FCLO Retreat Components.. 18 - 22
FCLO Retreat... 23 - 44
Journal.. 45

Part B—FCLO Crash Course on Communication

A Shout Out! From The Walkers... 49
How to Use this Communication Curriculum...................................... 50 - 51
Weekly Communication Schedule.. 52

Eight Week Sessions on Communication
Session 1 — Introduction and Orientation to Communication.................. 53 - 62
Session 2 — What Are You Talking About?.. 63 - 71
Session 3 — Fine-Tuning Your Communication Channels....................... 73 - 80
Session 4 — Avoiding Corrupt Communication.. 81 - 90
Session 5 — Tell Me What You Are Thinking .... 91 - 100
Session 6 — Do You Feel Me?... 101 - 108
Session 7 — I'm Sensing Something .... 109 - 114
Session 8 — Check Yourself... 115 - 125

[TABLE OF CONTENTS - Cont.]

Part C—FCLO Monthly Enrichment Program

A Word from the Walkers	129
How to Use the Monthly Marriage Enrichment Program	130 - 131
1st month — Talking Money with Your Honey	133 - 142
2nd month — Close Encounters of the Love Kind	143 - 151
3rd month — Labor of Love	153 - 160
4th month — Married with Children	161 - 168
5th month — Just a Friendly Matter	169 - 176
6th month — Power Plays	177 - 185
7th month — It's a Relative Thing	187 - 192
8th month — Time to Chill	193 - 200
9th month — Working People	201 - 207
10th month — Having Church	209 - 213
11th month — To Move or Not to Move	215 - 219
12th month — Our Covenant of Love	221 - 226
Walker marriage/family resources	229 - 231
Notes	232 - 237

[Drs. Clarence & Ja'Ola Walker]

Proverbs 24:3—" Through skillful and godly wisdom is a house, a life, a home, a family built and by understanding it is established on a sound and good foundation." (AMP)

Drs. Clarence and Ja'Ola Walker teach biblical principles to families, singles and youth across denominational and ethnic lines with a special burden for the African-American family. They are spiritually, professionally and experientially equipped for ministry and serve as excellent role models for married life. Their teaching is sound, biblical, down-to–earth, and practical in order that everyone can understand as the Holy Spirit teaches through them.

Combining their professional training, sound biblical principles, experience, and humor with the anointing of the Holy Spirit, Drs. Clarence & Ja'Ola Walker travel extensively sharing God's principles for successful marriage, victorious single living, and healthy relationships. The Walkers have appeared nationally on many radio and television programs including the *700 Club*, and they are featured speakers at conferences and seminars throughout the United States and the world.

Drs. Clarence and Ja'Ola Walker have been married and ministering together for over 33 years. They have two sons, Justin and Arthur.

Dr. Clarence Walker is a born-again servant of the Lord Jesus Christ. He received a Ph.D. in Biblical Counseling from Trinity Theological Seminary, a M.S.W. from Temple University, and a B.S.W. in Social Work from Eastern College. He earned a Graduate Certificate in Marriage and Family Therapy from the Marriage Council of Philadelphia and the University of Pennsylvania School of Medicine, Department of Psychiatry; Division of Family Study. He received additional training from the Minnesota Institute for Couples Communication. He was a professional marriage and family therapist in a private practice for twelve years.

Dr. Clarence Walker is also the pastor and founder of the Fresh Anointing Christian Center. He has also served as a founding elder, associate pastor, and minister of family and evangelism at various ministries. Dr. Walker is the author of two books: *Biblical Counseling with African-Americans and Breaking Strongholds in the African-American Family* published by Zondervan. He is a contributing author to *Biblical Strategies for a Community in Crisis, Called to Lead*, and *Prayer Time*. Dr. Walker has served as an adjunct professor at Eastern Baptist Seminary, and has received numerous awards and commendations for service to communities. Dr. Walker's dynamic and practical preaching as an evangelist has influenced the lives of many in this nation and in the Caribbean.

Dr. Ja'Ola Walker is the co-pastor of the Fresh Anointing Christian Center and a featured speaker at many conferences and seminars for women. She received an Honorary Doctorate of Divinity from Jameson Christian College, a M.Ed. in Counselor Education from West Chester State College, and a BA in Psychology from Eastern College. Dr. Walker received additional training from the Minnesota Institute for Couples Communication and Certified Parents Skills Inc. She is a contributing author to the book *Called to Lead* and has served as an adjunct professor at Eastern Baptist Seminary. Dr. Walker is the author of *The Eight Powers of a Woman*. Most importantly, she is a wonderful wife, a dedicated mother, and a loving friend and prayer partner.

[THE ABC's OF *FOR CHRISTIAN LOVERS ONLY*]

(An Affectionate Affair)

Begin your journey with the For Christian Lovers Only retreat. In this curriculum you will find everything you need to plan and execute a successful marriage retreat for couples in your community. There is information for pre-retreat publicity, retreat scheduling, and planning for teaching times and engaging activities for couples. The teaching component of the DVD featuring the dynamics of Pastor Walker and Dr. Walker will enlighten couples to rededicate themselves to the Lord and to each other. We recommend that each spouse have their own FCLO Participants Workbook.

(Building Blocks of Communication)

Couples are usually riding high after a marriage retreat; however, after a few weeks or sooner, many fall back into the same rut they were in before they attended. The goal of the eight week course is to stimulate and encourage healthy communication between spouses. This course should begin immediately after the retreat on a specific day and time and meet weekly without interruption. In the DVD, the Walkers provide momentum to each communication lesson by introducing the subject matter. Each lesson is taught by a layperson or ministry leader of a small group where directions are clear and easy to follow. Couples will learn the biblical and practical ways of communicating through words, body language, touch, written word, and action. This in-depth study will give each couple what they need to further their spiritual and emotional growth into the next level of teaching.

■ (Conflict Resolution)

After learning how to communicate, couples will need time to put what they learned to practice. By meeting together on a monthly basis for one year for teaching and accountability, married couples will be able to deal with the issues that are common to all marriages such as money, work, children, and so on. These small groups will give opportunities to couples to lead and teach their peers as they learn themselves. For each lesson, there is a real-life, humorous introduction for each session of conflict resolution.

[Straight talk to my brothers and men of God]

First, I want to commend you for choosing to participate with your wife in the F.C.L.O. curriculum, and I believe that your marriage will be blessed because of your decision. You are about to embark on a journey of learning. It is a journey that I have been on for more than 33 years with my wife and am still traveling. On this journey God's Word will be our map to help us get to our destination.

The responsibility for being a husband today is a challenging one, for there are forces at work in our society to redefine marriage and traditional family values. The result has been confusion about what it means to be a husband. Yet we know *God is not the author of confusion*. If you have been one of the brothers that have felt that confusion, be encouraged; you are not alone.

I believe God's Word, the Bible, is still the place where we must look to get clarity on our marital roles and responsibilities. Moreover, as Christian men, we are commanded in Scripture to *love our wives as Christ loved the church*. God has set the love standard very high that only with His power and grace can we ever hope to attain to it.

It is not a coincidence that you have decided to journey with us through this curriculum. Your steps have been ordered by the Lord and your path destined to come this way. The fact that you're open to teaching is an indication that the journey has now begun. Therefore take comfort in knowing that "He that hath begun a good work in you will perform it until the day of Jesus Christ."

Your Fellow Traveler,

Dr. Clarence Walker

[Straight talk to my sisters and women of God]

Blessings, my sister. I am so glad that you made the decision to go through this next year of the F.C.L.O. curriculum growing, learning and stretching. Your marriage is worth the time and investment. Be encouraged that God has a plan to prosper you and not to harm you. I am a witness that His Word works!

As God's children we have looked to the world for many years for direction about our roles and purpose as wives. We have mixed so much of what the world tells us that we have lost the wonderful vision that God has for Christian marriages. It's not working for us. Christians now have a divorce rate of 34% which is equal to non-Christians and higher than atheists.

We can't just do a little of the Word and take out what is uncomfortable for us. I challenge you to give God's Word a try. He created us. He understands the uniqueness of women, our vulnerability and our strengths. He knows under what conditions we will thrive, and He does not want you under someone's foot. He also set the authority system in the family for your protection. It's not just emotional, cultural, or psychological. There is a spiritual component to marriage that the world does not understand and has even been overlooked or misunderstood by some church folk.

When you do marriage God's way, it works because He watches over His Word to perform it. He makes it work. He often sets up systems that are opposite to the common sense of the world.

Begin praying now, my sister. Cover your home with prayer and believe God for healing, peace, unity, joy, love, and provisions. We are agreeing with you for wonderful things to happen in the next year. Be blessed.

Your servant in Christ,

Pastor Ja'Ola Walker

[THE SEVEN P's of RETREAT PLANNING]

I. PRAYER

Any major project on a mission to reclaim God's perfect plan for husbands and wives will take on repeated attacks from within (the spirit man) and without (the devil). The best defense from these attacks will be united and fervent prayer of those who endeavor to step into enemy territory and rescue those under the delusions of Satan.

II. PEOPLE

A planning committee is needed to meet on an average of twice a month leading up to weekly meetings the month before the retreat. Each role is vital and necessary to the successful execution of the retreat. Choose people with a heart for God's plan for marriage and ministry.

A. Publicity Coordinator – responsible for getting the announcements, radio, TV, e-mail, and print.

B. Registration Coordinator – selects hosting couples, responsible for the registration process and set up, collection of funds, keeping records and balancing of bills.

C. Prayer Coordinator – organize and set up prayer once a week for an hour for at least 2 months before the event.

D. Accommodation Coordinator – sets up power point presentation equipment, selects hotel/resort and the availability of piano and/or keyboard.

E. Equipment Coordinator – responsible for selection and set up of quality public address and microphone (headset) system.

F. Worship Leaders – lead devotions and mini concert on Saturday evening, plan music and lyrics, make decisions on musical instruments needed.

G. Program Director – makes announcements, gives directions, introduces each segment and keeps program moving by making adjustments as necessary.

H. Serenade Coordinator – contacts couples to prepare serenade before retreat.

I. Group Leaders – lead small groups of couples for discussion after the DVD. It would be helpful for them to meet beforehand to watch the DVD and read over the discussion questions.

III. PUBLICITY

In order for this retreat to be well attended, there needs to be excellent advertisement. Publicity should involve all forms of free media including public service announcements on the radio, on the television, and in the newspapers. Putting the information on your church website as well as bulletin inserts are effective means of getting the word out. A sample promotional flyer is included in the back of the leader's guide.

IV. PLACE

FCLO retreats should always be held at quality hotels or resort areas. In order to create the most effective environment for married couples, it is necessary to have aesthetic surroundings, recreational facilities, a banquet area, and a large conference room. Meals should be arranged at the hotel or resort so the group can stay together. Couples need to get away to a place that feels far from home, yet doesn't break the budget.

V. PAYMENT

The cost of the retreat is dependent on its location and amenities. We recommend a reasonable price that would include the accommodations, meals, registration fees, and packet materials. There should be a non-refundable deposit required to reserve a spot at the retreat as well as a late fee payment after the registration deadline. This will assist in the planning of how many couples will participate in the retreat.

VI. PRODUCTS

The main product of the retreat is the FCLO participant's guide which will be used throughout the entire FCLO program. This guide will be used for the retreat, the eight week communication program, and the monthly enrichment group.

VII. PARTICIPANTS

We recommend that FCLO Retreats have 25 to 50 couples for each retreat. With effective publicity participants may come from throughout the community. Participants should be encouraged to bring their Bibles and a special song, poem, or tribute for their mates during the Couples Serenade, in addition to providing couples with the list of what they need to bring to the retreat.

Come away, my lover, and
be like a gazelle or like a young
stag on the spice-laden mountains.

(Song of Solomon 8:14, NIV)

[THE RICHES OF A RETREAT]

Retreat comes from the Latin word *retrahere,* which means to draw back. A "drawing back" from the busyness of life gives opportunity for married couples to remember and rekindle the flame that first drew them together.

Many married couples find it difficult to get away because of the demands of their work, children, and ministry. However, without a Sabbath rest from the daily grind, couples find themselves short on temper, energy, and patience, which directly affects their spiritual, emotional, and physical intimacy. This retreat is a time of renewal and refreshment for love-starved, distracted couples. The best gift they can give to their children is time away to rejoice in the love of their lives.

Other reasons to take a retreat:

- Friendships forged with other couples
- Learning new skills even after decades of married life
- Acquiring new hope for failing marriages
- Remembering God's purpose and plan for marriage
- A safe environment in the fellowship of other believers
- Renewed confidence in marital roles

We recommend retreats take place in quality hotels, resort areas, campgrounds, or college campuses. If finances are tight for couples, the retreat can also take place at a church or a banquet facility for the Friday evening schedule where couples return home and resume the retreat for the Saturday schedule. The goal is to give the couples time for reflection, fellowship, and focusing on strengthening their relationship in an inviting environment.

[FCLO RETREAT SCHEDULE]

Time   **Friday's Events**

Time	
6:00 - 7:00 p.m.	Registration and Check-In
7:00 - 8:00 p.m.	*Dining with Your Darling*
8:00 - 8:15 p.m.	Orientation
8:15 - 9:15 p.m.	Couples Games
9:15 - 9:20 p.m.	Closing Prayer and Dismissal
9:30 - 10:00 p.m.	Orientation Meeting for Couple Group Leaders

Time   **Saturday's Events**

Time	
8:00 - 9:00 a.m.	Breakfast
9:00 - 9:15 a.m.	Devotions: *Love Songs to Jesus*
9:15 - 9:30 a.m.	Announcements and Introduction to FCLO video
9:30 - 10:30 a.m.	DVD Presentation Part I: Feelings
10:30 - 10:50 a.m.	Break into Discussion Groups
10:50 - 11:00 a.m.	Restroom Break
11:00 - 11:30 a.m.	DVD Presentation Part II: Respect
11:45 - 12:00 p.m.	Couples Exercise Part I (Pleasant Words)
12:00 - 12:15 p.m.	Couples Exercise Part I (Giving You What You Need)
12:15 - 12:30 p.m.	Feedback
12:30 - 1:45 p.m.	*Lovers Lunch*
1:45 - 2:00 p.m.	Resource Sales
2:00 - 5:00 p.m.	Free Time
5:00 - 6:30 p.m.	*Dining with Your Darling*
6:30 - 6:45 p.m.	Devotions: More Love Songs to Jesus
6:45 - 7:30 p.m.	*To Know You is to Love You* *The Do You Know Your Mate Game*—Games of Love
7:30 - 7:45 p.m.	Break

Time	Saturday's Events (cont.)
7:45 - 8:30 p.m.	Couples Serenade
8:30 - 8:40 p.m.	Couples Get Close (play Honorable Marriage while couples hold each other or sway together)
8:45 - 9:00 p.m.	Prayer—Couples Pray for each other and then closing prayer for group

Time	Sunday's Events
8:00 - 9:00 a.m.	Breakfast
9:15 - 9:30 a.m.	Devotions: *Love Songs to Jesus*
9:30 - 9:55 a.m.	Testimonies
9:55 - 10:25 a.m.	Couple Communication and Covenant Commitment Ceremony; "Surprise Your Mate" Gift
10:25 - 10:35 a.m.	Prayer and ministry
10:35 - 10:40 a.m.	Closing Song and Prayer
10:40 - 12:00 p.m.	Break — Checkout — return keys
12:00 - 1:00 p.m.	*Lovers Lunch* and Farewell

[FCLO RETREAT COMPONENTS]

FCLO Retreat
Registration Form

Husband's Name: _____

Wife's Name: _____

Address: _____

Home phone: _____ Cell: _____

Email address: _____

Church Affiliation: _____

Marriage Anniversary: _____ Length of time married: _____

[Emergency contact information:]

Name: _____ Phone number: _____

Special needs: _____
_____

[For staff use only]

Payment received on: _____

Total Amount due: _____

Form of payment: _____(cash) _____(check) _____(credit)

[Sign-up Forms for FCLO Communication Course]

Name:_____

Address: _____

Phone: _____ Email: _____

Best day/time to contact: _____

- -

Name:_____

Address: _____

Phone: _____ Email: _____

Best day/time to contact: _____

- -

Name:_____

Address: _____

Phone: _____ Email: _____

Best day/time to contact: _____

- -

Name:_____

Address: _____

Phone: _____ Email: _____

Best day/time to contact: _____

- -

Name:_____

Address: _____

Phone: _____ Email: _____

Best day/time to contact: _____

[WHAT COUPLES NEED TO BRING TO THE FOR CHRISTIAN LOVERS ONLY RETREAT]

Bibles

Pens

Comfortable clothing

Banquet attire (semiformal)

Clothing for sports activities

Be prepared to serenade your spouse with a song, poem, reading or tribute—each spouse should bring what they need. (Example: a soundtrack of the song you want to sing and a CD player)

There will be other resources available for purchase to strengthen your marriage.

[IDEAS FOR FREE TIME AT THE FOR CHRISTIAN LOVERS ONLY RETREAT]

Consider available activities when you book your resort or retreat location. If there is not much to do, bring games that small groups can play.

Set up a few group activities that the couples can sign up for if they are interested like (don't give too many options):

Basketball

Baseball

Football

Hiking

Volleyball

Horseback riding

Shopping

Swimming

Site tours

Please be sure to do research ahead of time so you can make the couples aware of the possible activities. Directions to tourist sites, prices and other details that they need should be included in their packet. They should make sure they have some time to rest and prepare for the evening activities.

Some people will want to rest or spend time with each other. This is fine as well—whatever they need to do to feel rested and enjoy each other.

[DINING WITH YOUR DARLING QUESTIONS]

1. What was the first thing you noticed about me when we first met?

2. What quality do you like about me the most?

3. If you had a chance to have any career in the world, what would it be?

4. What is your happiest memory of your childhood?

5. Is there anything that you think might increase our intimacy?

6. What do you think is our greatest strength as a couple?

7. Which of these describes how you see God: Friend, Father, Lover of your soul, Judge, Master, or other?

8. What is your favorite spiritual song? Why?

[FCLO RETREAT]

FRIDAY:

Registration (6:00 – 7:00 p.m.)

The set up for the registration table should be completed at least two hours before evening dinner. Make sure all signs are up to direct couples to the right tables and areas of the retreat. All pre-registration forms and payment records should be in order. All packets should be stacked and completed with all the content in order. The registration committee should check each notebook to make sure they are all complete with the following information:

- FCLO Participant's Guide
- Order forms for FCLO products
- Flyer announcing 8-week training
- Badge (ID)
- FCLO brochure
- Hotel and Resort brochure*
- Evaluation forms
- Church Information*
- Extra Bibles

Suggested items

[FRIDAY FCLO RETREAT]

DINING WITH YOUR DARLING (7:00-8:00 P.M.)

Have a few couples to host, greet, and direct the retreat couples to their tables. Play soft love music throughout the dinner; if possible, a romantic candlelit dinner is encouraged. Provide index cards with questions that couples can ask each other during their dinner. The décor color scheme of FCLO retreats is purple and pink. Be sure that the room is tastefully decorated to encourage an ambience of romance. Many times hotels will secure color decorations for you.

[Dining with Your Darling]

Husband: What new things did I discover about my wife this evening?

_____

_____

_____

Wife: What new things did I discover about my husband this evening?

_____

_____

_____

[FRIDAY FCLO RETREAT - Cont.]

ORIENTATION TO FCLO MOVEMENT (8:00-8:15 P.M.)

- Welcome the couples with enthusiasm and introduce yourself and the ministry sponsoring the retreat. Explain to the couples that this retreat is For Christian Lovers Only. Take a few minutes to describe the mission and the ABCs of the FCLO marriage curriculum.

- Encourage the couples to write in their retreat pages as much as necessary as a form of journaling this experience.

- After the orientation, instruct couples to look at their retreat schedule and make note of important times and location. Encourage the couples to take notes or journal through this journey. Emphasize punctuality, attendance, participation, and cooperation. Point out the major locations of meeting areas, restrooms, and recreational and eating facilities. Introduce any staff members that can be easily contacted should there be any questions or emergencies. Also mention any hotel/resort guidelines (i.e. parking) that need to be observed.

Husband: What goals do I hope to accomplish in this retreat?

_____

_____

_____

Wife: What goals do I hope to accomplish in this retreat?

_____

_____

_____

[FRIDAY FCLO RETREAT - cont.]

MATCH UP GAME AND CLOSING (8:15 – 9:15 P.M.)

- Encourage the participants to loosen up and introduce the Match Up Game. Have the couples pull out the sheet labeled Match Up from the retreat section of their FCLO Participant's Workbook.

- Instructions: Couples will go throughout the room and find someone who was born during the same month or on same day, has same number of children, received salvation on same day, has the same favorite colors or same age, etc…

- Have a prize for the winners of this game. You could give away romantic gifts such as candles, journals, sparkling cider, picture frames, etc.

- After closing prayer, encourage the couples to enjoy the resort and fellowship as well as check out the book table. Emphasize the need for everyone to be on time for breakfast the next morning.

Couples: What are the names of other couples we've met through the Match Up Game?

_____

_____

_____

[SATURDAY FCLO RETREAT]

BREAKFAST (8:00 – 9:00 A.M.)

Have breakfast promptly begin at 8:00 A.M. Instruct the hotel that breakfast will end at 9:00 A.M. to continue the program.

DEVOTIONS: Love Songs to Jesus (9:00 – 9:15 a.m.)

We suggest two couples to lead devotions who can engage an audience and have experience in worship leading. We recommend the following worship love songs:
- Oh, How I Love Jesus
- I Love You Lord, Today
- In Times Like These
- I Will Sing out a Love Song
- I Love You Lord and Lift My Voice
- I Keep Falling in Love with Him Over and Over
- I Really Love the Lord

ANNOUNCEMENTS AND INTRODUCTION TO FCLO VIDEO (9:15 – 9:30 A.M.)

Share with the couples the agenda for the day and any adjustments that may be necessary. Introduce the first part of the FCLO DVD. Instruct the couples to follow along the video and take notes on the Circle of Contentment worksheet provided in their participant's book.

DVD PRESENTATION I (9:30 – 10:30 A.M.) FEELINGS

During video presentation have group leaders prepare to set up for the dividing of the groups.

Husbands: What does your wife need from you? How can you meet her need?

_____

_____

_____

[SATURDAY FCLO RETREAT - cont.]

Wives: What does your husband need from you? How can you meet his need?

_____

_____

_____

DISCUSSION GROUPS (10:30 – 10:50 A.M.)

Give instructions for dividing groups. We have several options:

> **Option 1:** You can put everyone on your registered list before the retreat group. A, B, C, D or 1, 2, 3, or colors – you can put their group number, name or color on their packet or name tag.

> **Option 2:** If you have limited space you can just divide the group up into 4 or 5 even groups to each of the four corners of the room that they are close to. Use the front and back of the room if you need two additional locations. You want your groups to be about 10 – 14 people. If you have a larger group your smaller groups will have to be bigger.

Have someone keep time so the discussion groups will stay on schedule.

DISCUSSION QUESTIONS—SO WHAT DO YOU WANT FROM ME?

i. Women — What is the greatest emotional need you have?
ii. Men — What is the greatest ego need you have?
iii. Do you think you have clearly shared your need with your mate?
iv. Men — In what form does your partner like to receive affection (verbal, touch, gifts, or others?) What practical ways will you begin to do this or continue to do this?
v. Women — In what ways does your husband like for you to show him respect? What practical ways will you begin to do this or continue to do it?

Husbands: What is the greatest ego need you have? Do you think that you have clearly shared that need with your wife?

_____

_____

_____

[SATURDAY FCLO RETREAT - cont.]

Wives: What is the greatest emotional need you have? Do you think that you have clearly shared that need with your husband?

_____

_____

_____

Husbands: In what form does your wife like to receive affection (i.e. verbal, touch, gifts, or other?) What practical ways will you begin to do this or continue to do it?

_____

_____

_____

Wives: In what ways does your husband like for you to show him respect? What practical ways will you begin to do this or continue to do it?

_____

_____

_____

RESTROOM BREAK (10:50 – 11:00 A.M.)

DVD PRESENTATION II (11:00 – 11:30 A.M.) RESPECT PART II

Introduce second video presentation as before. Encourage couples to take notes.

[CIRCLE OF CONTENTMENT FOR WOMEN]

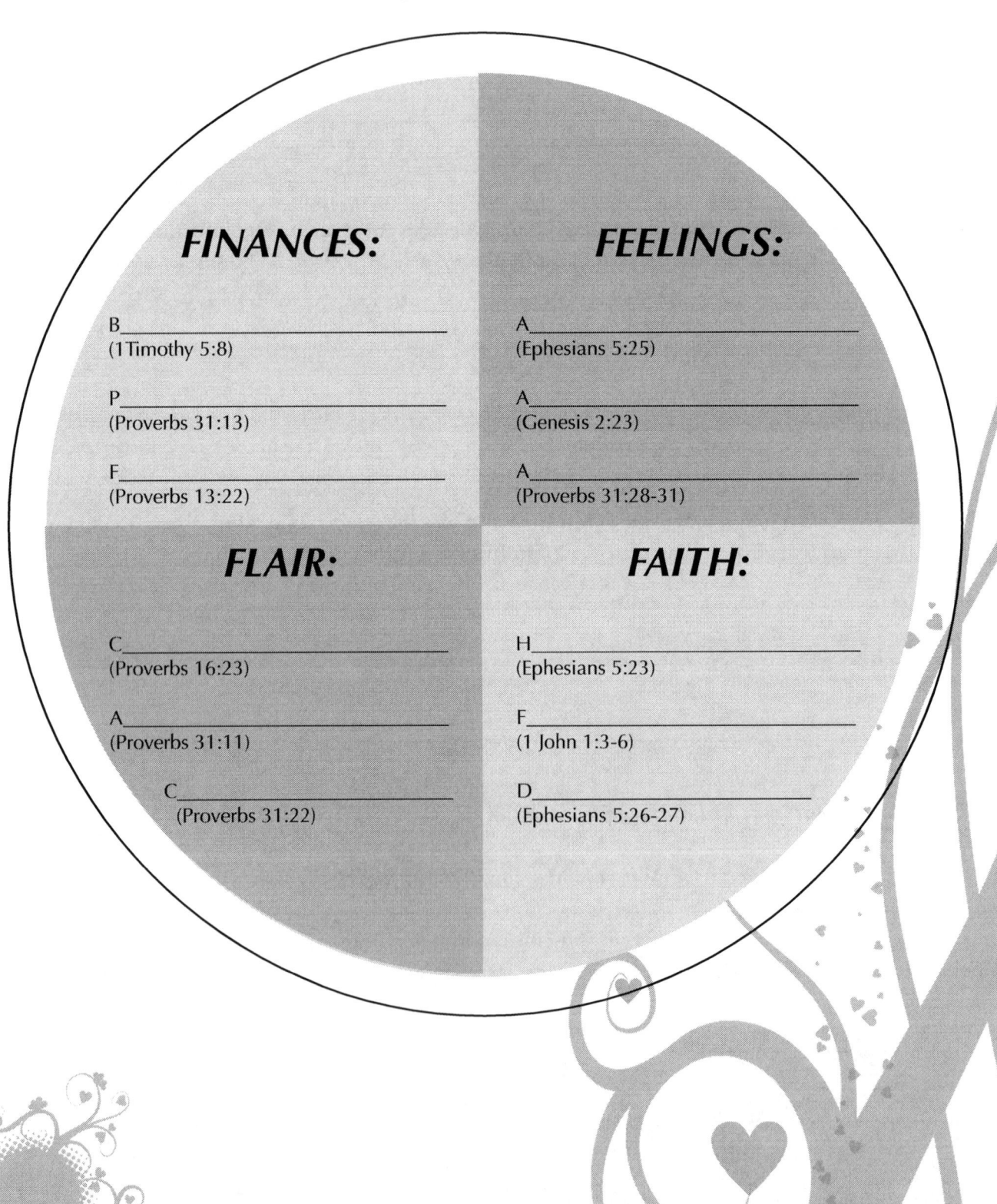

FINANCES:

B_____
(1 Timothy 5:8)

P_____
(Proverbs 31:13)

F_____
(Proverbs 13:22)

FEELINGS:

A_____
(Ephesians 5:25)

A_____
(Genesis 2:23)

A_____
(Proverbs 31:28-31)

FLAIR:

C_____
(Proverbs 16:23)

A_____
(Proverbs 31:11)

C_____
(Proverbs 31:22)

FAITH:

H_____
(Ephesians 5:23)

F_____
(1 John 1:3-6)

D_____
(Ephesians 5:26-27)

[CIRCLE OF CONTENTMENT FOR WOMEN]

FINANCES:

Basic Sustenance
(1 Timothy 5:8)

Personal Allowance
(Proverbs 31:13)

Future Inheritance
(Proverbs 13:22)

FEELINGS:

Affection/Femininity
(Ephesians 5:25)

Affirmation/Identity
(Genesis 2:23)

Approbation/Activity
(Proverbs 31:28-31)

FLAIR:

Communication
(Proverbs 16:23)

Aspiration
(Proverbs 31:11)

Complexion
(Proverbs 31:22)

FAITH:

Headship
(Ephesians 5:23)

Fellowship
(1 John 1:3-6)

Discipleship
(Ephesians 5:26-27)

[CIRCLE OF CONTENTMENT FOR MEN]

RICHES:

J_____
(Proverbs 16:26)

W_____
(Ecclesiastes 3:12-13)

F_____
(Proverbs 21:20)

RESPECT:

R_____
(Proverbs 31:26)

R_____
(Proverbs 12:4)

R_____
(1 Peter 3:1-3)

RELATIONSHIP:

S_____
(1 Corinthians 7:1-5)

H_____
(Titus 2:4)

S_____
(Proverbs 31:10-12)

RULING:

S_____
(Ephesians 5:23-24)

M_____
(1 Corinthians 11:3)

D_____
(Genesis 3:16)

[CIRCLE OF CONTENTMENT FOR MEN]

RICHES:

Job Employment
(Proverbs 16:26)

Work Enjoyment
(Ecclesiastes 3:12-13))

Fund Deployment
(Proverbs 21:20)

RESPECT:

Regard/Affection
(Proverbs 31:26)

Respect/Characterization
(Proverbs 12:4)

Reverence/Ordination
(1 Peter 3:1-3)

RELATIONSHIP:

Sexual Gratification
(1 Corinthians 7:1-5)

Home Domestication
(Titus 2:4)

Supportive Participation
(Proverbs 31:10-12)

RULING:

Spiritual Headship
(Ephesians 5:23-24)

Marital Leadership
(1 Corinthians 11:3)

Domestic Rulership
(Genesis 3:16)

[SATURDAY FCLO RETREAT - cont.]

COUPLES EXERCISE I - PLEASANT WORDS (11:45 – 12:00 P.M.)

*Show DVD for video instructions

Pleasant Words:
     Couples will face each other and the husband will begin. They are to share one line that is a compliment to their spouse, and the other spouse is only allowed to respond by saying, "Thank you. I receive that." After the husband shares, the wife responds in turn to give him a compliment, and then he will respond "Thank you. I receive that." They should go back and forth for at least five minutes. Examples for compliments: I think you are a wonderful mother, I think you are a great provider, I think you are sexy, etc…

Husband: What were the pleasant words you received from your wife?

_____

_____

_____

Wives: What were the pleasant words you received from your husband?

_____

_____

_____

[SATURDAY FCLO RETREAT - cont.]

COUPLES EXERCISE II - GIVING YOU WHAT YOU NEED (12:00 – 12:15 P.M.)

*Show DVD for video instructions

Giving You What You Need:
Each person will choose a topic from the Circle of Contentment worksheet that relates to their needs and choose the one that is the greatest for them. They will share with their partner and give one practical way their spouse can meet that need.

For example: A wife may choose "praise" with the section of emotional security. Her request to her husband, "This is my need, I would like for you to give me one compliment a day." He will respond in the affirmative to meet her need and then share his need and one request from her. They should commit to meeting that need immediately.

Husband: What need did your wife share with you? Name one way you will try to meet that need.

_____

_____

_____

Wife: What need did your husband share with you? Name one way you will try to meet that need.

_____

_____

_____

[SATURDAY FCLO RETREAT - cont.]

FEEDBACK (12:15 – 12:30 P.M.)

Encourage couples to share what they have learned and what practical ways they are going to put to practice what they know about their spouse. Afterward, have the couples refresh themselves before lunch and visit the resource table with tools to help build their marriage.

COUPLES: WRITE DOWN ANY THOUGHTS FOR FURTHER DEVELOPMENT.

_____

_____

_____

_____

LOVER'S LUNCH (12:30 – 1:45 P.M.)

- Play soft love music in background.
- A sit-down lunch with couples in the same discussion group is encouraged for further dialogue (or picnic-style outdoors if weather permitting and with hotel/resort cooperation).

RESOURCE SALES (1:45 – 2:00 P.M.)

Have a microphone to pass around and ask for volunteers to share their experiences and what they have learned. Give a few minutes for those who have questions.

[SATURDAY FCLO RETREAT - cont.]

FREE TIME (2:00 – 5:00 P.M.)

Encourage couples to rest or participate in recreational sports. Review the relevant guidelines for the games that include time, place, dress, etc. Make sure to have games available for the physically impaired to enjoy as well (i.e. musical chairs that could involve wheelchairs, charades, and other non-physical games). Remind the couples to pace themselves so they will be back for semi-formal dinner.

For those who want to participate in recreational sports:
- Assign a couple to supervise and lead games.
- Volleyball is recommended because it doesn't require a lot of equipment.
- Have every couple sign a waiver of suit to participate.
- Be sure to check any insurance coverage from the hotel/resort.
- Time the activity to give couples enough time to freshen up for dinner.

DINNER WITH YOUR DARLING (5:00 – 6:30 P.M.)

This candlelit dinner should again have a romantic décor. If possible, have sparkling cider or grape juice on each table. Soft romantic music should play in the background. Dinner should be served banquet-style and dress should be semiformal.

DEVOTIONS: MORE LOVE SONGS TO JESUS (6:30 – 6:45 P.M.)

Use songs from earlier devotions or introduce new ones.

[SATURDAY FCLO RETREAT - cont.]

GAMES OF LOVE (6:45 – 7:30 P.M.)

How Well Do I Know My Mate Game (similar to the Newlywed Game)

- Ask for three sets of volunteer couples who will play three games and answer three questions.
- Remove wives to a separate location where they can't hear their husbands being questioned.
- Husbands are asked three questions about their wives or marriage in general.
- Answers are written down on a sheet of paper in big handwriting so people can see their answers. Wives return to answer how they think their husbands responded. Afterward, husbands are removed and the wives are asked questions.
- Repeat another match with four other couples.

["HOW WELL DO I KNOW MY MATE" GAME]

Have a similar set up to the "Newlywed" Game Show.
Sample Questions: (pick three for the husbands and five for the wives)

How would your mate answer these questions?
Where did we go or what did we do on our first date?
Would your mate prefer to be: on a quiet beach, at a big gathering with lots of folk and fun, in a museum, or at the movies for a date out with you?
How would your mate describe themselves—gentle as a lamb, strong as a lion, free as a bird, smart as an owl, slick as a fox?
Does your spouse like surprise parties, or would he/she prefer to be in on the planning?
What is your spouse's favorite color?
What is your spouse's favorite pastime?
What is your spouse's favorite Bible verse?
Who will your spouse say is the role model couple for both of you?
Who will your spouse say is the couple for whom the two of you are role models?
What is the most loving thing your partner has ever done for you?

Greatest Introductions (First exercise)
- Have each husband introduce his wife and each wife her husband.
- Each one will hold hands, give their name, and introduce his/her partner as the greatest, best, or most of something. (For example, My name is Bill and this is my wife, Mary, the greatest cook in the world. My name is Mary and this is my husband, Bill, the most outstanding father ever.)

Husband: How did you feel about your wife's introduction of you?

_____

_____

_____

Wife: How did you feel about your husband's introduction of you?

_____

_____

_____

Eye Love You (Second exercise)
- Explain that when people love each other they have the look of love in their eyes.
- Instruct the couples to turn their chairs to each other, take their partners by the hand, get close, and tell their partners they love them with their eyes for two minutes.

Husband: Does speaking love with her eyes make a difference for you? Why or why not?

_____

_____

_____

_____

Wife: Does speaking love with his eyes make a difference for you? Why or why not?

_____

_____

_____

_____

[SATURDAY FCLO RETREAT - cont.]

Whispering Sweet Somethings (Third exercise)
- Instruct each couple to whisper sweet nothings—something romantic, sensual, and positive—to each other.
- Have the husbands go first and the couples speak back and forth to each other for about three minutes.

Husband: How did your wife's "Sweet Somethings" make a difference in your love for her?

_____

_____

_____

Wife: How did your husband's "Sweet Somethings" make a difference in your love for him?

_____

_____

_____

BREAK (7:30 – 7:45 P.M.)

[SATURDAY FCLO RETREAT - cont.]

COUPLES SERENADE (7:45 – 8:45 P.M.)
- Segment of program devoted to allowing couples to express their love for each other publicly in the form of a special song, poem, or tribute for their spouse.
- Give participating couples a five minute limit.
- Follow this time with playing "Honorable Marriage."
- 1st part of serenade should run approximately 45 minutes with the rest of the time devoted to the couples dancing to "Honorable Marriage."
- If acceptable to the ministry, couples should be encouraged to dance together (slow ballroom type dance). Play "Honorable Marriage" (music CD included in the packet). If your ministry doesn't believe in dancing, just have the couples stand and hug each other as the music plays.

Couples: How does serenading each other help you to appreciate each other more?

_____

_____

_____

BENEDICTION (8:45 – 9:00 P.M.)

[SUNDAY FCLO Retreat]

BREAKFAST (8:00 – 9:00 A.M.)

DEVOTIONS: LOVE SONGS TO JESUS (9:15 – 9:30 A.M.)

TESTIMONIES (9:30-9:55 A.M.)
    Devotional leaders can encourage couples to share how the Lord has blessed them through the weekend including what they have learned and how they have changed.

Husband's Testimony

_____
_____
_____
_____
_____
_____
_____

Wife's Testimony

_____
_____
_____
_____
_____
_____
_____

[SUNDAY FCLO Retreat]

COUPLES COMMUNION AND COVENANT CEREMONY (9:55-10:25 A.M.)
- A simple, but sacred ceremony with grape juice and matzo.
- Speak to the need for couples to examine their hearts (1 Corinthians 11).
- Give couples time for reflection if there is a need for confession and forgiveness.
- Have the husbands serve the wives and everyone take communion together.
- Have the couples restate their covenant to God and each other.

Suggestions for Communion Process

You need an officiator, either a minister or deacon to conduct services.

Purchase matzo or communion wafers, grape juice, and small cups ahead of time.

The elements should be prepared beforehand and covered.

Officiator should mention communion as a sacred closure event that is open to all believers.

Have someone read 1 Corinthians 11:23–28.

Officiator may give couples the opportunity to confess and/or ask forgiveness of each other, or he can pray a corporate prayer of forgiveness (optional).

Have each couple receive both elements.

Officiator will ask couples to hold the water or matzo in the air while stating, *"This is the body of our Lord Jesus Christ which was broken for you, eat ye all of it in remembrance of Him."*

Officiator will ask the couple to hold up the cup (optional: ask each couple to exchange their cup with their partner as a sign of unity). The officiator will state, *"The blood of our Lord Jesus Christ which was shed for you drink all of it in remembrance of Him."*

While cups are being collected, couples can sing hymns such as "Oh The Blood of Jesus," "Power in the Blood," "At the Cross," or other songs.

[SUNDAY FCLO Retreat]

FCLO Covenant
Read the covenant in phrases and have the couples repeat after you.

Husband: I covenant before the Lord to pray daily for my family and keep a pure heart before the Lord. I will ask Him to fill me with His Spirit, and to empower me to love my wife as He loves the Church. I will choose to forgive and by God's grace protect her, cherish her and meet her needs. I will fill my home with His Word, and His peace by loving God first, myself, and then honoring and regarding my wife.

Wife: I covenant to the Lord to pray for my family on a daily basis. I will ask the Lord to fill me with His love and empower me to respect my husband. I will use the words of my mouth to bring life and healing to my family. I will fill my home with His Word and His peace by loving God first, myself, and then honoring and regarding my husband.

Husband and Wife: (facing each other while holding hands)
As we journey through this life together we covenant to put the Lord first in our home. We will pray together and make time to speak life and build each other up. We will put on the armor of God and resist all attacks on our love, and by His grace and power we will be examples to the world of God's love for His Church.

Husband: Making this covenant before God and my wife leads me to…
_____
_____

Wife: Making this covenant before God and my husband leads me to…
_____
_____

CLOSING SONG AND PRAYER (10:25 – 10:35 A.M.)

Have the couples form a circle to sing songs that encourage unity of the Body of Christ and needing one another. Before dismissing with prayer remind the couples that the retreat is just the first step in the For Christian Lovers Only course. Encourage them to continue with the Communication course and provide a sign-up sheet for those who are interested in participating. End with the closing prayer.

BREAK AND CHECK OUT (10:40 –12:00 P.M.)

[JOURNAL]

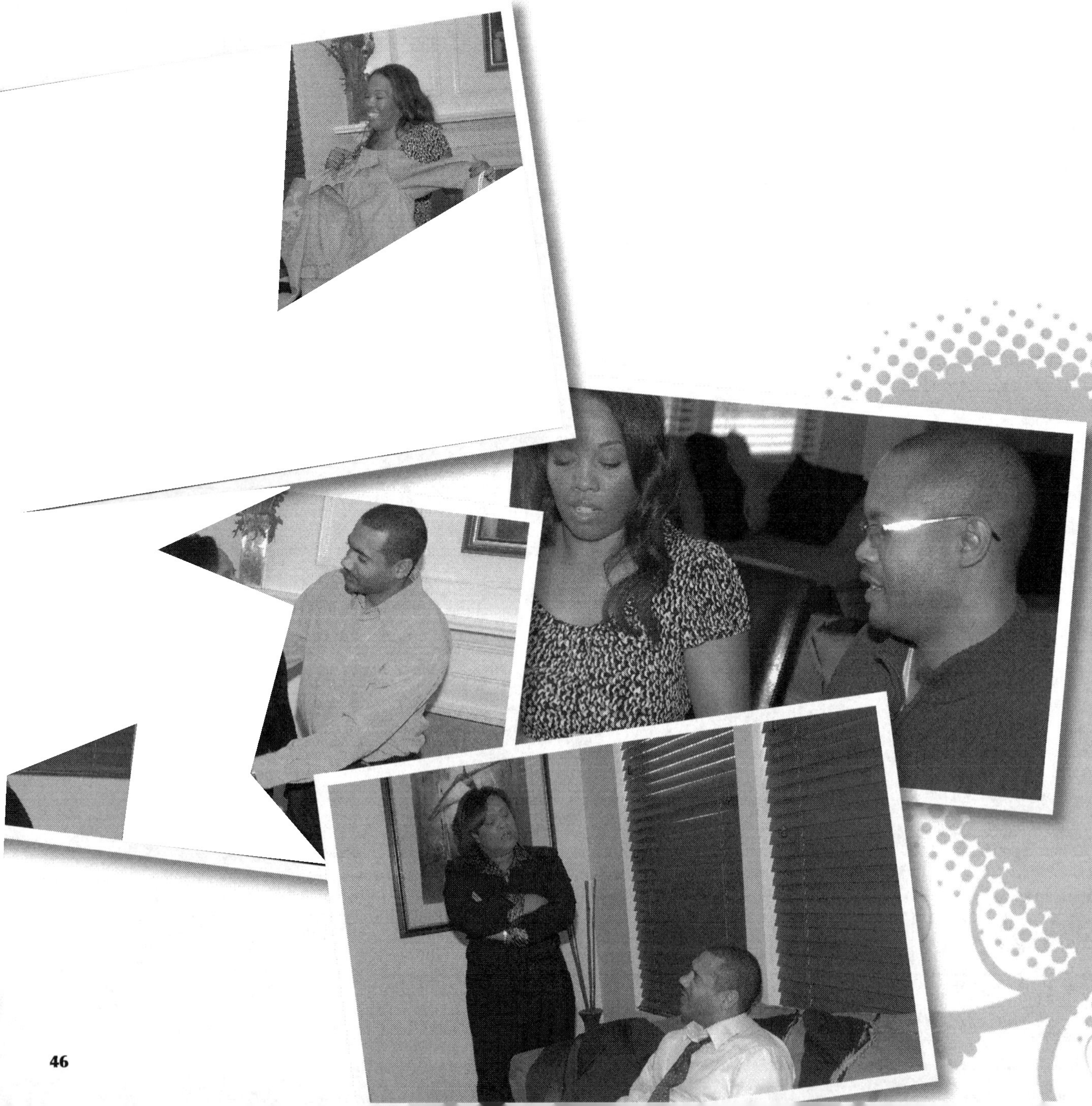

[8 WEEK COMMUNICATION COURSE]

I am my beloved's,
And my beloved is mine,
He who pastures his flock
among the lilies.

Song of Solomon 6:3, NASB

48

[A SHOUT OUT! FROM THE WALKERS]

We are very excited that you have chosen to go through this eight week communication training. Those couples with the best relationships take the time to improve, strengthen, and build upon the foundation of communication. We recommend that you also make the time and effort to attend the *For Christian Lovers Only* Retreat as it will set the tone of intimacy and closeness that provides the base for building your communication skills.

This course is necessary for couples who desire to talk "to" each other rather than talking "at" each other. Beginning with the basics of communication and building upon it with fine-tuning methods of conversation, dealing with dysfunctional interaction, and understanding the roles of thoughts, feelings, and discernment in couple interaction—everything couples need to successfully communicate with each other.

This journey will be fun, informative, and life-changing not just in your marriage, but it will have a trickle effect in all social relationships including parenting and work-related issues.

Once you learn the basics of communication, you and your spouse will be able to talk through any issue that comes up in your marriage. This will take work, commitment, determination, skills and the power of prayer.

God wants your spouse and you to stay in love through the long haul and not just be strangers passing in the night. Passions can last a lifetime as good communication will help you stay connected with each other, overcome conflict, and improve your sex life.

You're ready—let's get started.

[How to Use this Communication Curriculum]

1. Promote your upcoming couple enrichment program by using all available advertising venues. Your excitement about the training and communicating can be contagious to other couples as well.

2. Plan early to allow time to order participants' workbooks. We recommend that each couple have their own books.

3. We suggest that the registration include a small, non-refundable deposit to ensure a certain number of couples.

4. Classes are best in a private, quiet, clean, and comfortable setting in a room at a church, community center, or home where people are not cramped for space.

5. Each small group can number from three couples to a maximum of fifteen couples. Too many couples will make it difficult for the bonding that is necessary in a small group.

6. Remind all participants that this course requires an eight week commitment of attendance, participation, and homework.

7. It is most ideal for the husband and wife to attend together, but circumstances may keep one partner from attending. One spouse could attend, but there will not be the same level of benefit.

8. The group leader is a trainer, and there is preparation necessary to successfully lead the communication curriculum. We suggest the leader review the materials and each lesson before teaching. Prayer is a necessity before each session. Pray for each couple throughout the eight weeks so that they will have receptive hearts for healing and strength in their marriages.

9. We encourage the leader to write notes for better familiarization of the material. It is very important for the leader to connect with the audience and not just read through the material. We recommend the leader have excellent communication and teaching skills for the eight week session.

10. This course was written to make leading the couples as easy as possible. Instructions and directions for the leader are easy to read and communicate. Course curriculum for leader and participants are similar with the exception of the instructions for the leader.

11. Do the homework and assignments for yourself and your spouse for familiarity and incorporate the principles into your own lifestyle. This will help you draw from your own personal experience as you grow in your marriage and set the example for the other couples.

12. Your attitude is key—be friendly, warm, caring, confident, and exciting. You have a lot of important information to share that can heal people's lives.

13. Encourage sharing among couples; however, be careful of allowing more dominant or outspoken people to take over discussion groups. Maintain a pleasant, positive atmosphere. Immediately quiet any arguing or hostility between spouses or between group members. Speak privately to anyone who may be more of a distraction from the healing process for other couples.

14. These sessions are for teaching and training couples to learn specific knowledge and skills for communication. Do not attempt to give counseling or deliverance sessions. Couples with serious marriage problems, abuse, or emotional issues should be referred to their pastors, professional counselors, police, lawyer, or doctor.

15. Encourage the couples to continue on with the next FCLO step in the monthly marriage enrichment groups at the end of the eight week communication course.

16. Prayer is vital and especially necessary for marriage ministry. Be consistent in beginning and ending with prayer. A prayer guide has been provided for the leader, and prayers based on Bible passages have been provided for couples to pray aloud together at the end of each session.

[WEEKLY COMMUNICATION SCHEDULE]

Prayer

Welcome

Homework Feedback

DVD

Teaching Segment

Couple Exercises

Questions/Answers

Homework Assignments

Closure

Fellowship

[SESSION ONE]

Leader's Guide for Session One—
Introduction and Orientation to Communication

"The breakdown of marital communication was particularly helpful to us in getting on the same page regarding the adjustments we needed to make. The examples offered in the teaching revealed truths and kept it real so you don't feel like, 'Wow, we're the only ones that go through what we go through.'"

—Vincent & Teresa

Goals for Session One:
- **Glorify God through serving the body of Christ**
- **Familiarize couples with the course agenda**
- **Encourage fellowship among couples**

I. PRAYER (3 MINUTES)

It is always best to begin each session with prayer. During this time you can ask for prayer requests. The following Prayer Module uses the acronym A.C.T.S. to help the leader have direction for leading the other couples in prayer. This module begins each of the eight weeks and is optional for the leader to use or not to use depending on their comfort level.

Prayer Module (optional)
  A—Adoration (Begin with praise for who God is)
  C—Confession (Time to admit sin and seek forgiveness from God)
  T—Thanksgiving (Giving appreciation to God for all He has done)
  S—Supplication (Making requests to God)

II. WELCOME AND INVITATION (5 MINUTES)

Introduce yourself and welcome all the couples who are attending. Make sure all couples have name tags and encourage them to get to know each other better by participating in the Getting to Know You Exercise.

[SESSION ONE - Cont.]

III. GETTING TO KNOW YOU EXERCISE (10 MINUTES)

Have everyone turn to the Getting to Know You Exercise in the participant's workbook. Explain that they are to find other couples who have something in common with them and write their initials in the box. Give them ten minutes to complete this exercise.

IV. EXERCISE REFLECTIONS (5 MINUTES)

After the time has expired, ask a couple of volunteers to share what they have in common with other couples in the group. Encourage the couples in the group to get know each other better and support each other throughout the course.

V. SHOW DVD (5 MINUTES)

Play the DVD introduction to Session One.

VI. PURPOSE AND EXPECTATIONS OF FCLO TRAINING (10 MINUTES)

Explain to the couples that FCLO is marriage enrichment training for couples who want to grow spiritually and emotionally in their marriages. Have the couples turn to "Orientation Goals and Expectations" in their participant's workbook. Briefly review over the goals and expectations.

VII. OVERVIEW OF THE SESSIONS (10 MINUTES)

Have the couples turn to "Overview of Eight Week Communication Course" in their participant's workbook. Briefly review over the topics that will be covered in the next seven weeks. Encourage the couples to commit to being at each session as one builds upon another.

[SESSION ONE - Cont.]

VIII. QUESTION AND ANSWER (5 MINUTES)

Ask participants if they have any questions or comments regarding the curriculum.

IX. GOAL SETTING (15 MINUTES)

Have each couple turn to "Communication Goals for our Marital Relationship." Give the couples fifteen minutes to discuss the goals they want to establish for their marriage and write them in the book. Immediately afterwards give each individual two to three minutes to fill out the "Communication Evaluation Sheet."

X. HOMEWORK EXPLANATION (5 MINUTES)

Encourage everyone to do the homework as it is a vital part of the course. Point out how the homework should take more than fifteen minutes. For session one, have couples complete their communication goals for their marriage.

XI. CLOSURE (5 MINUTES)

For the first session, the leader will pray the following prayer aloud with their spouse. For the last seven lessons, encourage a different couple at each meeting to recite the closing prayer.

"Dear Heavenly Father, we pray that the words of our mouth and the meditations of our hearts be acceptable in Your sight. Fill our mouths with good things and let the law of kindness reign in our home. In Jesus' name, Amen."

XII. FELLOWSHIP (15 MINUTES)

We encourage light, healthy snacks to top off the study.

[GETTING TO KNOW YOU GAME]

FIND A COUPLE TO FILL IN THEIR NAMES:

- Married the same number of years _____
- Married in the same month _____
- Married in the same year _____
- Same first or last name _____
- Born in the same city and/or state _____
- Attended same schools _____
- Same number of children _____
- Children with same first and last names _____
- Spouses born in the same month _____
- Lives on the same side of town _____
- Wearing same clothing colors _____
- Same height _____
- Same make or model of vehicle _____
- Same number of years as a believer _____
- Same favorite book of the Bible _____
- Same favorite gospel song _____
- Same favorite verse of the Bible _____
- Same favorite food dishes _____
- Same spiritual gifts _____

[FCLO ORIENTATION GOALS AND EXPECTATIONS FOR COMMUNICATION COURSE]

PURPOSE: To enrich the marriage relationships of Christians through biblical principles

GOALS FOR COURSE:
- To glorify God through serving the body of Christ
- To improve communication, negotiation, and conflict resolution skills from a Biblical perspective
- To develop a support network for couples
- To facilitate fellowship of Christians across denominations

EXPECTATIONS:

1. Attendance
Both husband and wife are needed to attend all eight sessions. Each course has exercises that will require active participation from couples.

2. Punctuality
Because of the busyness of our culture, all sessions should begin and end promptly on schedule. Each couple should commit themselves to timeliness for all sessions.

3. Participation
In order to get the most out of the curriculum, participation is expected and desired from each couple. This can include helping with exercises, discussions, or closing prayer times.

4. Dress Attire
Couples should dress comfortably, casually, and appropriately for group participation and discussion.

5. Homework
Homework is scheduled after each lesson for review as well as for further development of subject for couples. Homework should take no longer than 15–30 minutes in one sitting. This small investment of time is necessary to build a foundation for a successful relationship.

[OVERVIEW OF EIGHT WEEK COMMUNICATION COURSE]

I. Orientation and Introduction
Session one is an opportunity for the couples to learn about what the communication course offers and requires of them as well as a time for fellowship and connection with other couples.

II. What Are You Talking About?
Session two will teach couples the art and definition of communication as well as the elements of communication. Couples will have the opportunity to put communication skills to practice.

III. Fine Tuning Your Channels
Session three will help couples understand how they can communicate in five different ways—verbal, body language, scriptwriting, actions, and touch.

IV. Crazy Couple Communication
Session four will reveal to couples how eight corrupt forms of communication can cause a break in their connection.

V. Tell Me What You Are Thinking
Session five teaches couples how their thinking affects their communication process.

VI. Do You Feel Me?
Session six takes couples into the world of their feelings, teaching them how to tune into their feelings and clearly communicate them.

VII. I'm Sensing Something…
Session seven introduces couples to the spiritual discernment and intuitive impressions of the communication process.

VIII. Check Yourself
Session eight reviews the couples' communication abilities and transitions them into the monthly sessions.

[COMMUNICATION GOALS FOR OUR MARITAL RELATIONSHIP]

1) _____
   _____

2) _____
   _____

3) _____
   _____

4) _____
   _____

5) _____
   _____

6) _____
   _____

7) _____
   _____

8) _____
   _____

[REFLECTIONS OF COMMUNICATION FOR GOAL SETTING EXERCISE]

1. Did you look at your mate the whole time? Yes___ No___
2. Did your spouse look at you the whole time? Yes___ No___
3. Did you interrupt your spouse at all? Yes___ No___
4. Did your spouse interrupt you at all? Yes___ No___
5. Did you criticize or put your spouse down at any point? Yes___ No___
6. Were you criticized or put down by your spouse at any point? Yes___ No___
7. Did you talk more than your spouse? Yes___ No___
8. Did your spouse talk more than you? Yes___ No___
9. Did you get distracted? Yes___ No___
10. Did your spouse seem distracted? Yes___ No___
11. Did you hold back on sharing your goals? Yes___ No___
12. Do you feel that your spouse listened to you? Yes___ No___
13. Do you feel like you listened to your spouse? Yes___ No___
14. Did your spouse ask you questions for better understanding? Yes___ No___
15. Did you ask your spouse questions for better understanding? Yes___ No___

[REFLECTIONS OF COMMUNICATION FOR GOAL SETTING EXERCISE]

1. Did you look at your mate the whole time?   Yes___   No___

2. Did your spouse look at you the whole time?   Yes___   No___

3. Did you interrupt your spouse at all?   Yes___   No___

4. Did your spouse interrupt you at all?   Yes___   No___

5. Did you criticize or put your spouse down at any point?   Yes___   No___

6. Did you talk more than your spouse?   Yes___   No___

7. Did your spouse talk more than you?   Yes___   No___

8. Were you criticized or put down by your spouse at any point?   Yes___   No___

9. Did you get distracted?   Yes___   No___

10. Did your spouse seem distracted?   Yes___   No___

11. Did you hold back on sharing your goals?   Yes___   No___

12. Do you feel that your spouse listened to you?   Yes___   No___

13. Do you feel like you listened to your spouse?   Yes___   No___

14. Did your spouse ask you questions for better understanding?   Yes___   No___

15. Did you ask your spouse questions for better understanding?   Yes___   No___

[BIBLICAL COMMUNICATION SKILLS]

What do the following Scriptures teach about communication between couples?

1. James 1:19
   _____
   _____

2. 1 Peter 3:8
   _____
   _____

3. Proverbs 18:13
   _____
   _____

4. Ephesians 4:29
   _____
   _____

5. Proverbs 13:2–3
   _____
   _____

6. James 3:5–10
   _____
   _____

7. Matthew 12:37
   _____
   _____

[SESSION TWO]

FCLO Leader's Guide for Session Two—
What Are You Talking About?

"My husband and I were helped most by the homework assignments. We particularly enjoyed making the collages for one another that expressed our love in a variety of ways. Using pictures and captions to speak words and convey messages, that otherwise go unspoken, gave my husband and me the chance to share our thoughts as never before."

— Craig & Melissa

Goals for Session Two:
- Help couples understand what communication is
- Give couples an opportunity to demonstrate good communication
- Facilitate fellowship between Christian couples
- Prepare couples for the next communication session

Resources needed: FCLO Participant's Workbook for each person, Bibles, pens or pencils, FCLO DVD (eight week, session two), at least two old magazines or newspapers per couple, glue, scissors, and construction paper.

I. PRAYER (3 MINUTES)

Always begin with opening prayer.
Ask for prayer requests.

Prayer Module (optional)
    A—Adoration (Begin with praise for who God is)
    C—Confession (Time to admit sin and seek forgiveness from God)
    T—Thanksgiving (Giving appreciation to God for all He has done)
    S—Supplication (Making requests to God)

[SESSION TWO - Cont.]

II. WELCOME (2 MINUTES)

Introduce yourself and welcome all the couples who are attending. Make sure all the couples have name tags.

III. HOMEWORK FEEDBACK (10 MINUTES)

Ask for a show of hands of couples who completed the homework from the last meeting. Have a few couples share their experience and what they learned from the homework. Encourage the couples to do the homework as part of the learning process of communication.

IV. SHOW DVD (5 MINUTES)

Play the DVD introduction before the teaching session.

V. TEACHING (30 MINUTES)

Part 1: What is communication?
Have couples turn to session two in their participant's workbook.

    Leader: "Why do we need to communicate as a couple?"
Give couples opportunity to share why they think communication is important.

    Leader: "Communication is probably the most important skill in your marriage. Couples who have any form of marital problems usually have negative communication skills regardless of their other problems. If a couple has good communication skills, they can resolve just about any issue that comes up in marriage."

    Leader: "What is the dictionary definition of communication?"
Read the following dictionary definitions of communication to the couples and have them write out key words that stand out to them.

        "Merriam-Webster's Dictionary defines communication as 'an act of transmitting and exchange of information or opinions, a message.'"

[SESSION TWO - Cont.]

Leader: "Now let's focus on how the Bible defines communication."
Assign the following scriptures for couples to look up and hold in place: Ephesians 4:29, Colossians 3:8, and Philemon 6

Have a couple read Ephesians 4:29.

"Do not let any unwholesome talk come out of your mouths, but only what is helpful for building others up according to their needs, that it may benefit those who listen." (NIV)

"Let no corrupt communication proceed out of your mouth, but that which is good to the use of edifying, that it may minister grace unto the hearers." (KJV)

Leader: "The Old Testament was originally written in Hebrew and the New Testament was in Greek. In Ephesians 4:29, 'Let no corrupt communication' is in the King James translation and reflects what Paul originally wrote. Paul wrote the word *logos* which means to speak something, a word spoken, an expression of intelligence, or a conversation. It is clear human language. Matthew 5:37, John 1:1, and Luke 24:17 have the same Greek meaning."

Instruct couples to fill in the words in their Participant's Workbook.

Have a couple read Colossians 3:8.

"But you must rid yourselves of all such things as these: anger, rage, malice, slander, and filthy language from your lips." (NIV)

"But now ye also put off all these; anger, wrath, malice, blasphemy, filthy communication out of your mouth." (KJV)

Leader: "Sometimes the KJV translators used the same word in English but it was a different word in the original language, so you get a slightly different meaning. The Greek word translated *communication* in this verse is *aischrologra* (Ahee-skrol-og-rah) which means shameful speaking, vile conversation, and filthy communications."

[SESSION TWO - Cont.]

Have a couple read Philemon 6.

"I pray that you may be active in sharing your faith, so that you will have a full understanding of every good thing we have in Christ." (NIV)

"That the communication of thy faith may become effectual by the acknowledging of every good think which is in you in Christ Jesus." (KJV)

Leader: "The Greek word translated for communication in this verse is *koinonia* (koy-no-nee-a) which means fellowship, partnership, participation, communion, having in common; this word related to action.

"The combined definition of communication from the Bible and dictionary is:

Communication is the participation of a husband and wife in giving and receiving messages concerning thoughts, feelings, discerning, sensing, and actions. In session three we will expand on these five channels of communication. But first we will go deeper into the elements that we use for communication as couples."

Part 2: How does communication work?

Leader: "Everyone has a general understanding of how communication works with the illustration of a phone. For example, you have a caller, a receiver, a phone (the means of communication), the message, and the meaning of the message."

*Instruct couples to fill in the blanks for the next section.

[SESSION TWO - Cont.]

Leader: "These are the five elements of communication:
1. The Sender - the person who sends the message
2. The Message - the communication sent by the Sender
3. The Receiver - the person to whom the message is sent
4. The Channel - the medium through which the message is sent
5. The Meaning - the interpretation and value of a message to the receiver

"The sender is the person 'sending' the message. There are five factors affecting the sender. They are:
- How they value themselves (self-image)
- How they value the listener
- Their spiritual, emotional, and physical well-being and maturity
- Their intelligence
- Their main type of communication skills"

Examples of sender elements of communication:
If the sender values themselves and the receiver, their message is most likely going to be more positive, and even if it is criticism, it will be more constructive with the goal of helping the person.

If the sender has a low self-image, they may make more negative assumptions about what the other person is thinking or doing. Some people with a low self-image find it difficult to look another person in the eye.

If they have a low view of the receiver, their message is most likely to be disrespectful in tone, attitude, or even body language.

Leader: "The message is the communication sent by the sender to the receiver. Factors affecting the message are:
- Was it a simple or complex message?
- Was it a long or short message?
- Was it a direct or indirect message?
- Was the message given in public or private?"

Examples of the message elements of communication:
"My dear husband doesn't seem to know what is funny and what is not. We all know that he likes to joke around since he thinks he's a comedian. But we all know that this is a very private matter and the utmost discretion is needed, so please excuse us while we handle this."

[SESSION TWO - Cont.]

A simple, short, and direct message given in private to the husband from the wife, "You are getting on my nerves and when we get home—heads will roll."

Leader: "The receiver is the person to whom the message is sent. They have the same factors as the receiver.
- How they value themselves (self-image)
- How they value the listener
- Their spiritual, emotional, and physical well-being and maturity
- Their intelligence
- Their main type of communication skills"

Examples of receiver elements of communication:
If the receiver has a positive self-image of themselves and the speaker, they may receive the message with positive assumptions—giving the speaker the benefit of the doubt where even negative messages are sometimes rationalized or excused by positive people.

If the receiver has a poor self-image of themselves and a low view of the speaker, they may receive the message with negative assumptions—they may jump to negative conclusions and read more into the message that wasn't there.

Leader: "The phone or channel is the medium through which the message is sent. There are four factors affecting the channel:
- Environment (happy, tense, angry, playful…)
- Senders awareness of the channels (how aware a sender is of the different methods of communicating)
- Kind of message the sender wants to communicate
- Kind of message the receiver will accept."

Examples of the channel element of communication:
If the environment is friendly, then the message "You are a pure fool" would be laughed at and seen in a playful way.

However, if the environment is hostile, then the message "You are a pure fool" could be fighting words.

[SESSION TWO - Cont.]

Leader: "The meaning is the interpretation or what it all means to the receiver. Factors affecting meaning are:
- Education level (can affect level of vocabulary skills and exposure to new ideas)
- Past experiences
- Culture (i.e. the different connotations of words such as *fool*)
- Gender (i.e. men and women may interpret the word *love* differently)"

Example of the message element of communication:
Many people have experienced being misunderstood by the receiver. Words spoken, tone, and attitude may be positive or innocent—but the cultural background and emotional and spiritual maturity of the receiver may misconstrue the message.

VI. COUPLES EXERCISES (20 MINUTES)

A. Talking Epistle

Ask someone to look up and read Psalm 45:1(KJV).

Leader: "The psalmist wrote, 'My tongue is the pen of a ready writer' to show that he was going to use his tongue like a writer uses a pen. The word 'epistle' means letter. For this exercise, each couple is going to use their words to write a letter to their partner."

"Each partner will speak to their spouse as if they were writing a letter. Then the partner will respond in a letter language. Each couple is to go back and forth with each other."

[SESSION TWO - Cont.]

Refer the couples to the example that is in their book.

For example:

> Dear Charles: I feel that we should set a specific time and day for us to meet together alone as a couple. I think we need to spend more time together.
> Lovingly Yours,
> Anita

> Dear Anita: I received your letter concerning us spending more alone time together. I think it's a great idea; although I feel like we need to work on our schedules.
> Sincerely,
> Charles

> Dear Charles: Thank you for your positive response. I believe that you want us to spend more time together as well, but you are concerned about our schedules. I can sit down tomorrow and write it out if that helps.
> Thanks,
> Anita

Give couples ten minutes to do this exercise.

B. Picture Me

Ask someone to look up and read Proverbs 25:11 (KJV). Pass out the magazine and newspapers to the couples.

Leader: "'A word fitly spoken is like apples of gold in pictures of silver' is the basis of this exercise. We are going to make a collage picture of our thoughts and feelings about our spouse with pictures, words, and symbols. Don't try to explain anything about your picture or comment on your spouse's picture."

Give couples 10 minutes to complete this exercise.

[SESSION TWO - Cont.]

VII. QUESTIONS AND ANSWERS (5 MINUTES)

Ask the couples if they have any questions about the definition and process of communication.

VIII. HOMEWORK ASSIGNMENT (5 MINUTES)

Explain to the couples that their assignment is to take the collages home and as soon as possible to sit down and discuss them together. They will exchange collages and tell their partners what messages they receive from them. After each person has a turn to explain, the other partner will comment on what they were trying to convey and if the interpretation was accurate. Afterward, the couple should complete their own "Assessing Your Communication Process" worksheet.

IV. CLOSURE (5 MINUTES)

Encourage a different couple at each meeting to give the closing prayer to include petitioning God's help in better communication between the married couples.

"Dear Heavenly Father, we thank You for the truth of Your Word that sets us free. Please forgive us from past negative speaking. We are grateful for the blood of Jesus that cleanses us from all unrighteousness. As we speak life in our home, please strengthen us to obey your Word. In Jesus' name, Amen."

V. FELLOWSHIP (15 MINUTES)

We encourage light, healthy snacks to top off the study.

72

[SESSION THREE]

Leader's Guide for Session Three—
Fine-tuning Your Communication Channels

"The interaction with the other couples was fun and allowed us to get to know them better. We particularly found helpful the session on the importance of listening to your partner and echoing back what you heard. We also learned different ways of expressing our feelings. By consistently applying the excellent concepts that we have learned in the Communication Classes, our marriage and relationship have been strengthened."

— Bob and Pat

Goals for Session Three:
- Help couples understand the five channels of communication
- Teach couples the five channels of communication
- Lead couples to discover how they use the five channels
- Prepare couples for the next communication session

Resources needed: FCLO Participant's Workbook for each person, Bibles for each couple, pens or pencils, and the FCLO DVD (eight week, session three).

I. PRAYER (3 MINUTES)

Always begin with opening prayer.
Ask for prayer requests.

Prayer Module (optional)

A—Adoration (Begin with praise for who God is)
C—Confession (Time to admit sin and seek forgiveness from God)
T—Thanksgiving (Giving appreciation to God for all He has done)
S—Supplication (Making requests to God)

II. WELCOME (2 MINUTES)

Introduce yourself and welcome all the couples who are attending. Make sure all the couples have name tags.

[SESSION THREE - Cont.]

III. HOMEWORK FEEDBACK (10 MINUTES)

Ask for a show of hands of couples who completed the homework from the last meeting. Have a few couples share their experiences and what they learned from the homework. Encourage the couples to do the homework as part of the learning process of communication.

IV. SHOW DVD (5 MINUTES)

Play the DVD introduction before the teaching session.

V. TEACHING (30 MINUTES)

Part 1: What are the five channels of communication?

    Leader: "Please turn to session three in the Participant's Workbook."

    "One way couples communicate is verbally or speaking in conversation. This is an essential part of communication. Our words can have a tremendous impact on ourselves and others. Let's get more understanding about what the Bible teaches us about our words."

Make sure each couple has a Bible so they can look up and read the following Scriptures. After each Scripture, have the couple reading it tell the group what the Scripture reveals about words.

[SESSION THREE - Cont.]

A. Matthew 12:37—your words will bring condemnation or justification

B. Proverbs 6:2—your words can hold you captive

C. Proverbs 15:1—your words can stir up anger

D. Proverbs 18:8, Psalm 64:13 and 26:2—your words can wound

E. Proverbs 16:24—pleasant words are sweet and can make the heart glad

F. Proverbs 12:18, 15:4—words can affect your health

G. Proverbs 18:21—words can release life or death

H. Acts 15:15, 2 Peter 1:21, and Hebrews 13:7—God used the *logos* for verbal communication

Leader: "We also communicate through body language with actions, gestures, movements, postures and dress."

"What are some examples of body language that couples speak to each other and what do you think they mean?"

Examples of body language:

Smiling	Crossed arms
Laughter	Wringing hands
Winking	Clenched fists
Relaxed Posture	Raised eyebrows

Leader: "Christ was God's thoughts, feelings, and ideas becoming flesh. He represented God's innermost thoughts expressed through the body because the Word (*logos*) became flesh. What do we learn from John 1:14?"

*Have couples look up and read John 1:14. Afterward, explain that Christ is the Word in bodily form; therefore, He is the body language of the Godhead.

[SESSION THREE - Cont.]

Leader: "We can also communicate to each other through writing and pictures such as through letters, cards, or notes. This form of communication is most often neglected and abandoned by couples once they get married, even though it was frequently used during courtship."

"Paul used written communication for the churches in Acts 15:30 and Colossians 4:16."

"Another channel we communicate with is through our actions."

*Have the couples share with you any ideas about how they communicate through actions. Use the following examples to lead conversation:

Action: Failing to do something that you said you would do
Communicates:

Action: Taking over a troublesome task for your mate
Communicates:

Action: Never making time for each other
Communicates:

Action: Constantly forgetting special days
Communicates:

Action: Taking care of the house
Communicates:

Action: Leading in spiritual disciplines (i.e. prayer, Bible study)
Communicates:

Leader: "How does Genesis 40:6–7 reveal communication through body language?"

*Have couples look up and read Genesis 40:6–7 to reveal how body language is a form of communication.

[SESSION THREE - Cont.]

Leader: "The last form of communication is through touch. What are the positive examples of how couples communicate through touch and what do they communicate?"

*Have couples share examples of positive touching.

Examples of positive touching for married couples:

Kissing   Holding hands   Sexual intercourse   Hugs   Massage

Leader: "What are some negative examples of touch and what can it speak to their partner?"

*Have couples share examples of negative touching.

Examples of negative touching for married couples:

Hitting   Shoving or pushing away   Grabbing

Leader: "How do the following Scriptures (Solomon 1:2, 2:6) demonstrate communication through touch?"

*Have the couples look up the references, read the Scriptures, and share what each reveals for what touching communicates.

Song of Solomon 1:2—Let him kiss me with the kisses of his mouth: for thy love is better than wine. KJV

Song of Solomon 2:6—His left hand is under my head, and his right hand doth embrace me. KJV

Song of Solomon 2:6—My lover's left hand is under my head, and his right arm holds me tight. NCV

[SESSION THREE - Cont.]

VI. COUPLES EXERCISES (20 MINUTES)

A. Word for Word Exercise

*Have each couple turn to face their partner. The husband should begin by picking a category in the physical, emotional, mental, or spiritual. For example, he could say "mental" and then say a positive word that describes his wife in that area like "thoughtful." The wife should then respond to the husband's same category and say something like "intelligent."

Allow ten minutes and then ask the following questions:

Leader: "How many had to really think about the words they were going to use? Did anyone not use a word for fear of how their partner would be affected?

"This exercise forces you to really think about what you are going to say with one word. You will avoid certain words because of how they would impact your spouse. It demonstrates the biblical principle of how life or death is in the power of the tongue.

"It also illustrates Proverbs 10:19 in that the more words we use, the more opportunity there is to sin. So as couples we must learn to shorten our conversations and think about the best words to use to communicate and the impact they will have on our partners.

B. Body Notes Exercise

Leader: "In this exercise, you will go back to the last discussion you had with your spouse, but you will communicate it using only your body gestures, postures, and motions similar to a game of Charades. Try to communicate your side of the story. Choose who will go first, and the other person will observe and only take notes. They should write until they have understood what their partner has demonstrated. Then switch places and repeat the process."

[SESSION THREE - Cont.]

After ten minutes, have the couples return as a group and ask the following questions:

Leader: "How many were able to complete this exercise? How many found it difficult?

"The note taker is forced to pay attention to their partner's body language, and the actor had to use their body productively to get the message across. In this exercise, which of the five senses became primary?" (Answer: sight)

"We must become more aware of how we communicate messages to our spouses with our bodies. We can also develop the habit of writing notes as an alternative way of communicating."

VII. QUESTIONS AND ANSWERS (5 MINUTES)

Ask the couples if they have any questions about the five channels of communication.

VIII. HOMEWORK ASSIGNMENT (5 MINUTES)

Have the couples turn to the homework assignment in their Participant's Workbook.

"TOUCH OF CLASS"
Explain to the couples that they are to give their spouse a gentle five minute massage of the shoulders, hands or feet. Allow the spouse receiving the massage to choose which area is to be massaged. Husbands should begin first. Explain that there should be no sex, but wink or smile so that they will know that you are kidding.

"ACT OF HONOR"
Explain that they should pick one action to do for their spouse that will communicate a positive emotion such as love, contentment, or appreciation. They are to do it without talking, touching, using body language, or note-writing. It should be an action that will communicate a positive emotion to the spouse (examples are: gifts, doing a household chore that they normally don't do, etc.)

[SESSION THREE - Cont.]

*HUSBAND — My one small thing that I will do for the coming week that will communicate a positive emotion such as love, contentment or appreciation to my wife is:*_____

_____

*WIFE — My one small thing that I will do for the coming week that will communicate a positive emotion such as love, contentment or appreciation to my husband is:*_____

_____

IX. CLOSURE (5 MINUTES)

Encourage a different couple at each meeting to give the closing prayer to include petitioning God's help in better communication between the married couples.

"Dear Heavenly Father, we pray that as we study your Word, it will bring truth in our hearts that will be spoken out of our mouths. We pray that we would be vessels of honor that reflects Your glory in our bodies so that we can be a blessing to others. In Jesus' name, Amen."

X. FELLOWSHIP (15 MINUTES)

We encourage light, healthy snacks to top off the study.

[SESSION FOUR]

Leader's Guide for Session Four—
Avoiding Corrupt Communication

"This class helped us to practice positive communication even during times of disagreements. It helped us to see ourselves and laugh at ourselves in a non-threatening manner. We realized our own areas of weaknesses that need to be strengthened in order to have more effective communication. It was also helpful to see other couples going through what we were experiencing and to see them communicate this reality in a humorous manner."

— Kenyatta & Shamalia

Goals for Session Four:
- Enable couples to identify negative communication patterns
- Teach a more productive and effective communication from a biblical perspective
- Help couples understand the nature of good biblical communication based on Ephesians 4:29

Resources needed: FCLO Participant's Workbook for each person, Bibles for each couple, pens or pencils, and the FCLO DVD (eight week, session four).

I. PRAYER (3 MINUTES)

Always begin with opening prayer.
Ask for prayer requests.

Prayer Module (optional)
    A—Adoration (Begin with praise for who God is)
    C—Confession (Time to admit sin and seek forgiveness from God)
    T—Thanksgiving (Giving appreciation to God for all He has done)
    S—Supplication (Making requests to God)

[SESSION FOUR - Cont.]

II.   WELCOME (2 MINUTES)

Introduce yourself and welcome all the couples who are attending. Make sure all the couples have name tags.

III.   HOMEWORK FEEDBACK (10 MINUTES)

Ask for a show of hands of couples who completed the homework from the last meeting. Have a few couples share their experience and what they learned from the homework. Encourage the couples to do the homework as part of the learning process of communication.

IV.   SHOW DVD (5 MINUTES)

Play the DVD introduction before the teaching session.

V.   TEACHING (30 MINUTES)

Part 1: What does Ephesians 4:29 reveal about corrupt communication?

*Have all the couples turn to Ephesians 4:29 and read the verse together.
"Let no corrupt communication proceed out of your mouth but that which is good to the use of edifying that it may minister grace unto the hearers." (KJV)

Leader: "Let's look at the original meaning of the major words used in this text; all of the New Testament was written in Greek."

1) *Corrupt* comes from the Greek word *sapros*.

Corrupt means rotten, worthless, bad, putrid vegetable or animal substances which have gone bad. Rotten is that which is spoiled, broken down in its composition, decayed, and has become inferior and unpleasant. It denotes that which is worn out by age and no longer fit for use.

[SESSION FOUR - Cont.]

2) *Communication* comes from the Greek word *logos*.

Communication is what is spoken, human utterance, speech, or language, expression of reasoning, or intelligence.

3) *Good* comes from the Greek word *agathos*.

Good is the benefit, useful, profitable, of good constitution or nature, excelling in respect, pleasant, agreeable, upright, or honorable.

4) *Edifying* comes from the Greek word *oikodome* (*oy-kod-om-may*).

Edifying means to build, refers to building as a process as well as that which is built, namely a house or dwelling, architecture, structure, an act which facilitates one's growth, comes from two words—*oikos* (meaning home) and *demosto* (meaning build)—thus, to build a home.

5) *Minister* comes from the Greek word *didomi* (*did-o-mee*).

Minister means to give, bestow, adventure, offer, deliver, to show, or to yield.

6) *Grace* comes from the Greek word *charis*.

Grace means to rejoice, favor, acceptance, kindness, benefit, thanks, and gratitude. It is a favor without expectation of return, pleasure, graciousness that which affords joy, pleasure, delight, loveliness, good will, and service.

Leader: "So when you put the expanded Greek version of each word in that verse, Ephesians 4:29 would read like this:

"Let no corrupt, rotten, worthless, bad communication proceed out of your mouth but that which is good, beneficial, useful, profitable, excelling in respect, pleasant, agreeable, upright, or honorable; to the use of edifying, building up that it may minister, give, bestow, offer, deliver, grace, favor, acceptance, kindness, benefit, thanks, and gratitude unto the hearers."

[SESSION FOUR - Cont.]

Leader: "From Ephesians 4:29 we learn that we should not allow putrid, inferior, rotten, or worn out words proceed out of our mouths but that which is good.

"There are seven forms of corrupt communication which many couples engage in."

1. Double Mind Binding (James 1:8)

This form of communication is used when the sender sends two conflicting messages in which the receiver gets confused and often put in a no-win situation.

Examples:
A wife complains, "You never hug me or caress me." The husband goes to hold her hand, but she pulls away and says, "Don't touch me."

Spouse yawns indifferently while telling their mate how much they love them.

Biblical Cure: James 4:8—purify your hearts. Sinful hearts make us double minded, hypocritical, defensive and deceptive. We should yield ourselves to the Lord on a daily basis and ask Him to let the words of our mouths and the meditations of our hearts be acceptable in God's sight. A pure heart is honest with God and will be honest with itself and others.

2. False Prophesying (Proverbs 18:13, Deuteronomy 18:22)

This form of communication is used when the sender engages in trying to read the mind and forecast the feelings of their spouse.

Examples:
Spouse tells their mate what they are thinking without giving them the opportunity to speak. This can make the other spouse angry and often shuts them down from attempting to communicate.

Biblical Cure: Instead of trying to read the other person's mind, be quick to hear according to James 1:19 (slow to speak, quick to hear, and slow to anger, NIV). Spouses need to understand that "out of the abundance of their heart the mouth speaks"—Matthew 12:34, KJV) and by listening long enough to their partner, they will know what is in their heart.

[SESSION FOUR - Cont.]

3. Holy Ghosting (John 16:8, Romans 8:33, 34)

This form of communication is used when a spouse tries to bring guilt and conviction to the heart of their mate. Sometimes a husband or wife will play the martyr attempting to invoke guilt as they suffer through the relationship.

Examples:
- **Silence** / not speaking to spouse
- **Tears** / crying
- **If it weren't for me** / self-righteous mode in which one takes credit for the relationship
- **Comparison** / comparing spouse with someone they admire as a better role model
- **Martyr** / spouse wanting to invoke guilt as they suffer through the relationship

Biblical Cure: Matthew 7:1—judge not so that you will not be judged. Remember that the Holy Spirit has the job of convicting of sin, not man. By repenting of pride and self-righteousness, each spouse allows the Holy Spirit to convict of sin and bring restoration.

4. Cursing (James 3:8-10, Psalm 62:4)

This form of communication is the act of putting negative labels on the other spouse. Using words to criticize or put a mate down to make them feel of little worth, insignificant, and of low esteem.

Examples:
"You are so stupid."
"What can't you do anything right?"

Biblical Cure: Repent of anger or bitterness and begin the practice of esteeming and blessing your mate based on James 3:10, NIV (out of the same mouth come praise and cursing…this should not be). Ask the Lord to help you control your words and yield to the Holy Spirit when He leads you to speak blessings or perhaps to not speak at all.

[SESSION FOUR - Cont.]

5. Spiritual Sword Fighting (Ephesians 6:17, Proverb 12:18)

This form of communication is when couples use the Word of God to mutually cut each other up. The Bible is the Sword of the Spirit to be used against Satan, not against flesh and blood.

Examples:
"You are supposed to love me like Christ loved the church!"
"Well, you are supposed to submit to me as unto the Lord!"

Biblical Cure: Recognize that the Word of God is the Sword of the Spirit and is a weapon against the devil according to Ephesians 6:12, 17, NIV ('for our struggle is not against flesh and blood, but against the ruler, against the authorities, against the powers of this dark world and against the spiritual forces of evil in the heavenly realms…the sword of the Spirit, which is the word of God').

6. Preaching (Romans 2:21, 2 Corinthians 4:5)

This form of communication is in which a spouse goes on a long, moral discourse and speech about what the mate ought to be doing. It often involves self-righteous generalizations and one's personal philosophy about right and wrong.

Example:
"The reason we are struggling with this problem is because you refuse to do…and you ought to be doing…and I think that….and you should….because I say that…"

Biblical Cure: Repentance and self-examination based on Romans 2:21 in which believers focus on improving their relationship with God and growing to accept others the way that God made them.

[SESSION FOUR - Cont.]

7. Stumbling Blocking (Romans 14:13)

This form of communication is when one spouse attempts to get the other off track by changing the subject or introducing an irrelevant subject to the conversation.

Example:
"We need to deal with your spending habits."
"Sure, but what about the fact that you are spoiling our daughter?"

Biblical Cure: When a spouse tries to trip their partner up by playing mind games or pretending they don't understand what the other is trying to communicate, it only leads to hurt and frustration. According to Romans 14:13, "No man [should] put a stumbling block or an occasion to fall in his brother's way" (KJV).

8. Interrupting (1 Peter 3:8)

This form of communication doesn't allow one partner to finish what they are saying.

Example:
"I think the dog…"
"You don't need to worry about it."
"But what I'm trying to say is that…"
"I said it's taken care of!"

Biblical Cure: Interrupting each other is in direct opposition to 1 Peter 3:8 where believers are called to be courteous to each other.

VI. COUPLES EXERCISES (20 MINUTES)

Instruct the couples to complete the "Crazy Couple Communication Identification Exercise." First have them do a self-analysis and then switch papers for their spouse to check over as well.

[SESSION FOUR - Cont.]

VII. QUESTIONS AND ANSWERS (5 MINUTES)

Ask the couples if they have any questions about the five channels of communication.

VIII. HOMEWORK ASSIGNMENT (5 MINUTES)

Each couple should practice overcoming their negative communication practices and document when each makes an effort. If a spouse makes an effort at least three times in the next week, then couples should decide and agree on a reward that they both will enjoy.

IV. CLOSURE (5 MINUTES)

Encourage a different couple at each meeting to give the closing prayer to include petitioning God's help in better communication between the married couples.

"Dear Heavenly Father, help us to lay aside every sin and weight which attempts to hinder our marriage. We bless Your name as You have begun a good work in each of us and You will perform it until the day of salvation. In Jesus' name, Amen."

V. FELLOWSHIP (15 MINUTES)

We encourage light, healthy snacks to top off the study.

[CRAZY COUPLE COMMUNICATION IDENTIFICATION EXERCISE]

Identify the negative communication patterns in your marriage. Write the name of the spouse who regularly communicates in the described pattern. Write both names if both spouses practice it or write "not applicable" if neither spouse practices it.

Who?

1. Criticizes, labels, or name-calling _____

2. Cries when they don't get their way _____

3. Gives the silent treatment when angry _____

4. Uses Scripture to make spouse feel guilty _____

5. Give two confusing or conflicting messages _____

6. Always speaks for other spouse, attempts mind reading _____

7. Changes the subject when confronted or talks about something negative _____

8. Tries to make spouse feel like they are unstable or they have the facts wrong _____

9. Talks to spouse in a patronizing or parental manner _____

10. Interrupts when spouse is speaking _____

11. Ignores spouse while they are talking or won't answer directly _____

12. Becomes overly emotional or hysterical in conversation _____

13. Never admits fault or denies that anything is wrong _____

14. Wants to be distant, not affectionate, or enjoys space _____

[CRAZY COUPLE COMMUNICATION IDENTIFICATION EXERCISE]

Identify the negative communication patterns in your marriage. Write the name of the spouse who regularly communicates in the described pattern. Write both names if both spouse practice it or write "not applicable" if neither spouse practices it.

Who?

1. Criticizes, labels, or name-calling _____

2. Cries when they don't get their way _____

3. Gives the silent treatment when angry _____

4. Uses Scripture to make spouse feel guilty _____

5. Give two confusing or conflicting messages _____

6. Always speaks for other spouse, attempts mind reading _____

7. Changes the subject when confronted or talks about something negative _____

8. Tries to make spouse feel like they are unstable or they have the facts wrong _____

9. Talks to spouse in a patronizing or parental manner _____

10. Interrupts when spouse is speaking _____

11. Ignores spouse while they are talking or won't answer directly _____

12. Becomes overly emotional or hysterical in conversation _____

13. Never admits fault or denies that anything is wrong _____

14. Wants to be distant, not affectionate, or enjoys space _____

[SESSION FIVE]

Leader's Guide for Session Five—
Tell Me What You Are Thinking

"We've learned that communication is more than just words or speaking. Basically it's everything we do. We've always considered ourselves as having a pretty good marriage, but after the sessions we talk and enjoy each other's company more. We still occasionally review the exercises and handouts."

— Elder Anthony and Phyllis

Goals for Session Five:
- **Enable couples to understand the three categories of thinking in communication**
- **Help them understand how their thinking process affects communication**
- **Facilitate group interaction between couples**
- **Prepare them for the feeling side of communication**

Resources needed: FCLO Participant Workbook for each person, Bibles for each couple, pens or pencils, and the FCLO DVD (eight week, session five).

I. PRAYER (3 MINUTES)

Always begin with opening prayer.
Ask for prayer requests.

Prayer Module (optional)
    A—Adoration (Begin with praise for who God is)
    C—Confession (Time to admit sin and seek forgiveness from God)
    T—Thanksgiving (Giving appreciation to God for all He has done)
    S—Supplication (Making requests to God)

II. WELCOME (2 MINUTES)

Introduce yourself and welcome all the couples who are attending. Make sure all the couples have name tags.

[SESSION FIVE - Cont.]

III. HOMEWORK FEEDBACK (10 MINUTES)

Ask for a show of hands of couples who completed the homework from the last meeting. Have a few couples share their experiences and what they learned from the homework. Encourage the couples to do the homework as part of the learning process of communication.

IV. SHOW DVD (5 MINUTES)

Play the DVD introduction before the teaching session.

V. TEACHING (30 MINUTES)

Leader: "For session five, we will look at how our thinking as individuals affects our communication as couples. Let's look at a conversation between a husband and a wife."

Wife asks, "Honey, did you set the trash out?", but she's thinking *I know you didn't because you never do.*

Husband responds, "No, but I'll get to it," but he's thinking *I am tired of you reminding me as though I am some irresponsible child.*

Leader: "Communication between married couples is heavily affected by the thinking patterns of the individuals. Couples must be aware of thinking statements in their communication. This includes:

Have couples refer to their guide for the listing.

Thoughts	Wants	Expectations
Impressions	Imaginations	Deductions
Ideas	Opinions	Assumptions
Beliefs	Conclusions	Wishes
Desires	Convictions	Aspirations
Philosophy	Evaluation	Interpretation
Assessment	Need	Intention

[SESSION FIVE - Cont.]

Leader: "Thinking statements will have one of the above words. For example:"

I think you're angry. (thought, conclusion)

I believe that husbands should be more affectionate. (belief, conclusion, philosophy)

I get the impression you don't want to talk to me. (impression, evaluation, interpretation, assessment)

I assume that you don't love or care for me. (assumption, opinion, conclusion)

I wish you would talk to me sometimes. (wish, desire, expectation, want, need)

I am going to work to improve our relationship. (intention, desire)

Leader: "Thinking patterns usually fall into three types: conclusive, interpretive, and expressive."

*Have couples fill in the blanks as you discuss the three thinking patterns.

Leader: "What is a conclusive thinking pattern? Conclusive thinking comes to a conclusion without knowing all the facts or information from the other spouse—it's a dead end. Unfortunately, most couples communicate with this thinking pattern.

Examples of conclusive thinking:

You don't care about me. (conclusion)
You did that to get back at me. (assumption, opinion)
Women should never question their husbands. (belief, philosophy)
I know that you reject me. (conclusion)
If you really loved me, you would do what I asked. (conclusion)

"Each of these demonstrate a pattern of thinking based on ideas, beliefs, assumptions, imaginations, opinions, and conclusions. Couples should be careful about coming to conclusion thinking prematurely because it can be foolish thinking according to Proverbs 18:13."

[SESSION FIVE - Cont.]

*Ask couples to share how they feel when someone comes to a conclusion without hearing all the facts. Keep it to one or two responses.

*Have a volunteer look up and read Proverbs 18:13, "He that answereth a matter before he heareth it, it is a folly and shame unto him." KJV

Leader: "The Hebrew translations give us a more in-depth meaning:

a. answereth — *shuwb* (*shoob*) is to return, to turn away, or give back to be given back.

b. matter — *dabar* is word, speech, or saying

c. folly — *ivveleth* (*iv-vehleth*) is to act foolish and silly

d. heareth — *shama* is to hear intelligently, to give undivided listening attention, to understand what one has heard, to get knowledge and gain new knowledge"

Leader: "This verse shows how conclusive thinking can bypass the communication process and goes right to the answer. However an interpretive thinking pattern tries to get knowledge by examining the merits before coming to an answer.

Examples of interpretive thinking:

I have been thinking about what you said.
I get the impression from your body language that you are angry with me.
I thought about what you said and interpret it to mean you need more space; is that correct?

"Each of these examples is based on impressions, interpretations, deductions, evaluations, and assessments."

[SESSION FIVE - Cont.]

Have a volunteer look up the following verses and write out what words or phrases in the Scripture represent interpretive thinking.

Leader: The Bible encourages interpretive thinking in the following verses:

a. 1 Corinthians 11:28 — examine
b. Psalm 119:95 — consider
c. Proverbs 23:7 — thinking
d. Proverbs 4:26 — ponder
e. Hebrews 11:11 — considered
f. Isaiah 1:18 — reason

Leader: "The expressive thinking pattern is a way for the speaker to express their thoughts to their spouse.

Examples of expressive thinking pattern:

I wish you would talk to me more often.
I need some time to myself.
I want us to be closer and more intimate.
I desire to make love more frequently.
I intend to rest this evening.
I expect loyalty from my spouse.

"Each of these examples demonstrates needs, wants, desire, expectations, wishes, dreams, or intentions."

Have a volunteer look up I Kings 2:19.

Leader: "This verse shows that Bathsheba expressed a desire and a petition that Solomon received and responded to.

"What can we learn about the differences about conclusive, interpretive, and expressive thinking?"

[SESSION FIVE - Cont.]

Expressive thinking is used for the thoughts the speaker sends about his or her needs.

Interpretive thinking is used for thoughts to understand and gain meaning from the speaker's message.

Conclusive thinking is the results and conclusions that the couple comes up with after they have shared their interpretive and expressive thinking.

VI. COUPLES EXERCISES (20 MINUTES)

What do you think? Exercise

Instruct couples to turn to "What do you think?" worksheet. For this exercise, couples should read each of the ten sentences and determine the type and category of thinking. Once everyone has completed the form, go over the answers and give ten points for each correct answer.

VI. QUESTIONS AND ANSWERS (5 MINUTES)

Ask the couples if they have any questions about the three ways of thinking and how each one can affect their communication.

VII. HOMEWORK ASSIGNMENT (5 MINUTES)

Tape-A-Talk

Tape-A-Talk—each couple will record a discussion concerning some disagreement or issue they have with each other. Afterwards they will listen to the conversation and fill in the Tape-A-Talk worksheet in the participant's workbook.

[SESSION FIVE - Cont.]

The "I's" Have It

Each couple will sit facing their spouse. One of them will begin by making an "I" statement, such as, "I am bored right now" or "I want you to be close." Each one is to reciprocate with an "I" statement so that the conversation might follow this example:

Husband: "I am bored."

Wife: "I am interested."

Husband: "I want to talk to you."

Wife: "I've been unavailable."

Continue this pattern for five minutes.

IX.   CLOSURE (5 MINUTES)

Encourage a different couple at each meeting to give the closing prayer to include petitioning God's help in better thinking in their communication between each other.

"Dear Heavenly Father, we thank You that the weapons of our warfare aren't carnal but mighty through the Father for the pulling down of mental strongholds. We lay down every plan, assumption, or system of thought that resists the Holy Spirit, and we choose to serve You. In Jesus' name, Amen."

X.   FELLOWSHIP (15 MINUTES)

We encourage light, healthy snacks to top off the study.

[What do you think? Exercise] (Answer sheet)

Instruct couples to turn to "What do you think?" worksheet. For this exercise, couples should read each of the ten sentences and determine the type and category of thinking. Once everyone has completed the form, go over the answers and give ten points for each correct answer.

	Type	Category
1. I expect loyalty from my spouse.	Expectation	Expressive
2. You don't care for me.	Conclusion	Conclusive
3. I get the impression that you're angry.	Impression	Interpretive
4. I want you to talk to me more.	Desire	Expressive
5. I would love it if we had more intimacy.	Need	Expressive
6. You are not even trying to fix our relationship.	Assumption	Conclusive
7. You seem down and depressed today.	Impression	Interpretive
8. I am the best thing that ever happened to you.	Assumption	Conclusive
9. I think you are jealous of your sister.	Impression	Interpretive
10. We need to get spend more time alone.	Desire	Conclusive

[What do you think? Exercise]

Instruct couples to turn to "What do you think?" worksheet. For this exercise, couples should read each of the ten sentences and determine the type and category of thinking. Once everyone has completed the form, go over the answers and give ten points for each correct answer.

	Type	Category
1. I expect loyalty from my spouse.	_____	_____
2. You don't care for me.	_____	_____
3. I get the impression that you're angry.	_____	_____
4. I want you to talk to me more.	_____	_____
5. I would love it if we had more intimacy.	_____	_____
6. You are not even trying to fix our relationship.	_____	_____
7. You seem down and depressed today.	_____	_____
8. I am the best thing that ever happened to you.	_____	_____
9. I think you are jealous of your sister.	_____	_____
10. We need to get spend more time alone.	_____	_____

LIST TO CHOOSE FROM (SOME ARE USED MORE THAN ONCE):

Conclusion	Need	Assumption
Expressive	Desire	Expectation
Conclusive	Interpretive	Impressive
Impression		

[TAPE-A-TALK]

Record or tape a discussion concerning some disagreement or issue with your partner. Afterwards play the conversation and follow the instructions below.

1. Identify the conclusive statements and the speaker.

Statement *Speaker*

_____ _____

_____ _____

_____ _____

_____ _____

2. Identify the interpretive statements and the speaker.

Statement *Speaker*

_____ _____

_____ _____

_____ _____

_____ _____

3. Identify the expressive statements and the speaker.

Statement *Speaker*

_____ _____

_____ _____

_____ _____

_____ _____

[SESSION SIX]

Leader's Guide for Session Six—
Do You Feel Me?

"In the early years of our marriage, my husband and I used to get angry with each other about how we 'felt' about something. It was as though it was wrong or bad just because one of us felt a certain way. Once we learned that our feelings were neither right nor wrong, it released us to accept each other's feelings, yet control how we expressed our feelings."

— Marshall and Crystal

Goals for Session Six:
- To enable couples to understand the difference in thinking and feeling.
- To help them be more sensitive to their own layered feelings and those of their partner
- To prepare them for next week's session

Resources needed: FCLO Participant's Workbook for each person, Bibles for each couple, pens or pencils, and the FCLO DVD (eight week, session six).

I. PRAYER (3 MINUTES)

Always begin with opening prayer.
Ask for prayer requests.

Prayer Module (optional)
    A—Adoration (Begin with praise for who God is)
    C—Confession (Time to admit sin and seek forgiveness from God)
    T—Thanksgiving (Giving appreciation to God for all He has done)
    S—Supplication (Making requests to God)

[SESSION SIX - Cont.]

II. WELCOME (2 MINUTES)

Welcome all the couples who are attending. Make sure all the couples have name tags.

III. HOMEWORK FEEDBACK (10 MINUTES)

Ask for a show of hands of couples who completed the homework from the last meeting. Have a few couples share their experiences and what they learned from the homework. Continue to encourage the couples to do the homework as part of the learning process of communication.

IV. SHOW DVD (5 MINUTES)

Play the DVD introduction before the teaching session.

V. TEACHING (30 MINUTES)

Leader: "For this teaching segment we are going to focus on feelings, and they can affect communication between couples. Many couples have difficulty distinguishing between their thinking from their feelings."

*Direct couples to the list in their workbook.

Feelings include being:

Happy	Angry	Glad	Bitter	Contented
Surprised	Depressed	Discouraged	Pleased	Irritable
Excited	Hateful	Joyful	Outraged	Jubilant
Compassionate	Worried	Timid	Fearful	Hurt
Shocked	Anxious	Frustrated	Sad	Lonely

Leader: "Feelings in and of themselves aren't necessarily good or bad. For example, 'rejoicing' can be good or evil according to 1 Corinthians 13:6 in rejoicing in iniquity or rejoicing in truth."

*Assign select Scriptures to couples to read and have them tell you what emotions are being described.

[SESSION SIX - Cont.]

A. Describe the biblical examples of emotion:

God the Father
Numbers 11:10—(anger)

Jeremiah 31:3—(love)

God the Son
Isaiah 53:3—(sorrow, grief)

Matthew 9:36—(compassion)

God the Holy Spirit
Ephesians 4:30—(grief)

Galatians 5:22—(love)

Leader: "We were created in God's image and we have feelings like God, but because of our sin nature our feelings can easily move into the negative. Even as Christians we must be aware of our negative feelings and how they can affect our communication.

"Can feelings turn into sinful actions? Paul writes of 'laying aside bitterness, wrath, anger, evil speaking, and malice'—these things directly affect our communication. Most of these issues are a form of anger or the result of improperly handled anger.

"What do the following Scriptures teach about anger?"

James 1:19 — slow to anger; anger doesn't work the righteousness of God

Ephesians 4:26 — don't sin in your anger; don't let the sun go down on your anger

Proverbs 15:1 — a soft answer turns away anger, but a harsh word stirs up anger

[SESSION SIX - Cont.]

Leader: "Couples need to share their feelings in the form of 'I' feeling statements. For example:

I am angry.   I am worried.
I am disappointed. I am excited.
I am afraid.   I am hurt.

David was the master of 'I' statements:

I am sorrowful. (Psalm 69:29)
I am full of heaviness. (Psalm 69:20)
I am afraid. (Psalm 119:120)
I am afflicted. (Psalm 88:15)

"David took responsibility for his emotions and feelings. He didn't say, 'You made me' rather 'I am.' This is one of the reasons he was a man after God's own heart (notice heart, not mind). David was in touch with his heart, his emotions, and feelings. He wasn't only God aware, he was self aware.

"Without open communication between our spouses, misunderstandings can occur. For example, in 1 Samuel 1:12-17 there is a miscommunication in the interaction between Hannah and Eli."

And it happened, as she continued praying before the LORD, that Eli watched her mouth. Now Hannah spoke in her heart; only her lips moved, but her voice was not heard. Therefore Eli thought she was drunk. So Eli said to her, "How long will you be drunk? Put your wine away from you!"

But Hannah answered and said, "No, my lord, I am a woman of sorrowful spirit. I have drunk neither wine nor intoxicating drink, but have poured out my soul before the LORD. Do not consider your maidservant a wicked woman, for out of the abundance of my complaint and grief I have spoken until now." (NKJV)

[SESSION SIX - Cont.]

VI. COUPLES EXERCISE—WHAT DO YOU FEEL? (20 MINUTES)

Leader: Have the couples turn to "What Do You Feel?" exercise in the participant's workbook. Instruct couples to get into a group with other couples and complete the worksheet.

VII. QUESTIONS AND ANSWERS (5 MINUTES)

Leader: Ask the couples if they have any questions about the feeling part of communication.

VIII. HOMEWORK ASSIGNMENT (5 MINUTES)

Leader: Instruct the couples that they are to keep a "feeling" diary for six days. There are two worksheets for each spouse in the participant's guide. They are also to prepare for the next lesson by reflecting on times when they sensed something was wrong with their spouse without the other one sharing with them.

IX. CLOSURE (5 MINUTES)

Encourage a different couple at each meeting to give the closing prayer to include petitioning God's help to better express their feelings to each other.

"Dear Heavenly Father, we thank You that we were created with feelings so we could love You with all our heart, mind, and soul as well as love each other. Help us to bring our feelings under the control of the Holy Spirit so that we can delight ourselves in You. In Jesus' name, Amen."

X. FELLOWSHIP (15 MINUTES)

We encourage light, healthy snacks to top off the study.

[What Do You Feel?]

Read the following ten statements and check either a feeling or thinking statement.

	Feeling	Thinking
I feel like my spouse really doesn't care.	_____	_____
I'm tired of being nagged all the time.	_____	_____
I am feeling that you are satisfied with this new job.	_____	_____
You are angry with me.	_____	_____
That hurts when you do that.	_____	_____
I am hopeful about our new level of communication.	_____	_____
I am very disappointed that we didn't discuss this issue.	_____	_____
It frightens me to see that much anger in a person.	_____	_____
I don't want to be this way.	_____	_____
I feel so warm and happy when you are here.	_____	_____

1. You are feeling lonely because you haven't spent much time with your spouse. What should you do?

    a. Give him the silent treatment so he will notice you.
    b. Occupy your time with other things outside of the home.
    c. Say "I am feeling lonely" to your spouse.
    d. Discuss your loneliness with an old flame.

2. You are angry because your spouse wouldn't listen to your point of view in an argument. What should you do?

    a. Punch a wall or slam a door.
    b. Leave the house.
    c. Pray and talk out your anger with God and your spouse.
    d. Talk to a spiritual mentor about your anger.

What are the potential consequences of each?

[FEELING DIARY]

DAY ONE
Today, I am feeling _____ because _____

_____

DAY TWO
Today, I am feeling _____ because _____

_____

DAY THREE
Today, I am feeling _____ because _____

_____

DAY FOUR
Today, I am feeling _____ because _____

_____

DAY FIVE
Today, I am feeling _____ because _____

_____

DAY SIX
Today, I am feeling _____ because _____

_____

My feeling diary for this week shows that:

_____

_____

_____

_____

[FEELING DIARY]

DAY ONE
Today, I am feeling _____ *because* _____
_____

DAY TWO
Today, I am feeling _____ *because* _____
_____

DAY THREE
Today, I am feeling _____ *because* _____
_____

DAY FOUR
Today, I am feeling _____ *because* _____
_____

DAY FIVE
Today, I am feeling _____ *because* _____
_____

DAY SIX
Today, I am feeling _____ *because* _____
_____

My feeling diary for this week shows that:
_____
_____
_____
_____

[SESSION SEVEN]

Leader's Guide for Session Seven—
I'm Sensing Something

"The FCLO communication training has truly been a blessing to us, both individually and as a couple on so many levels. It has inspired us to examine ourselves personally and spiritually for the fulfillment of our role as husband and wife. Our marriage is a true testimony of how God can turn any situation around and use it for His glory, if only we are willing."

— Jay & Monica

Goals for Session Seven:
- Enable couples to understand discernment in communicating with their spouse.
- Help couples become more sensitive to their own layered feelings and those of their spouse

Resources needed: FCLO Participant's Workbook for each person, Bibles for each couple, pens or pencils, and the FCLO DVD (eight week, session seven).

I. PRAYER (3 MINUTES)

Always begin with opening prayer.
Ask for prayer requests.

Prayer Module (optional)
- A—Adoration (Begin with praise for who God is)
- C—Confession (Time to admit sin and seek forgiveness from God)
- T—Thanksgiving (Giving appreciation to God for all He has done)
- S—Supplication (Making requests to God)

[SESSION SEVEN - Cont.]

II.   WELCOME (2 MINUTES)

Introduce yourself and welcome all the couples who are attending. Make sure all the couples have name tags.

III.   HOMEWORK FEEDBACK (10 MINUTES)

Ask for a show of hands of couples who completed the homework from the last meeting. Have a few couples share their experiences and what they learned from the homework. Continue to encourage the couples to do the homework as part of the learning process of communication.

IV.   SHOW DVD (5 MINUTES)

Play the DVD introduction before the teaching session.

V.   TEACHING (30 MINUTES)

Leader: "Discernment is the sensing intuition or premonition that comes from the spirit of a man. Believers of the Lord Jesus Christ tap into the spiritual realm through the Holy Spirit and God's Word.

Discernment can help couples with communication by enabling them to pick up on the deeper issues behind thinking and feeling. Some problems remain unresolved unless the deeper issues of discernment are dealt with.

For example, a spouse that is displaying angry emotions, thinking angry thoughts, or showing angry body language may have a deeper issue of hurt and a wounded spirit. With the help of the Holy Spirit, a loving spouse can discern the true issue and discuss it with the offended partner."

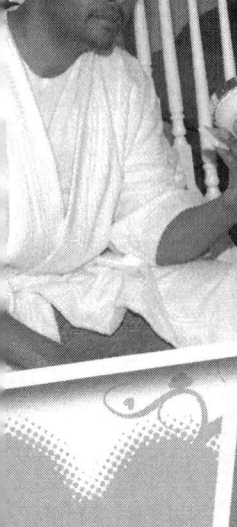

[SESSION SEVEN - Cont.]

Leader: "This is what comes out of the spirit of a man:

Intuitions   Perceptions   Revelations   Reflections
Hunches   Premonitions Instincts   Hurts
Anguish   Feelings   Enlightening

What do the following scriptures reveal about the responses of the spirit?"

Have the couples look up the following Scriptures and share what they reveal about the responses of the spirit.

1. Genesis 4:8, John 13:21, Daniel 2:3—it can be troubled

2. Deuteronomy 2:30—it can be hardened

3. 1 Samuel 1:15, 1 Kings 21:5—it can be sorrowful

4. 1 Chronicles 5:26, Acts 17:13—it can be stirred

5. Haggai 1:14—it can search

6. Proverbs 15:13, 17:26—it can be breached, hurt

7. Isaiah 29:24—it can make a mistake

8. Proverbs 17:22, Proverbs 18:14—it can sustain an infirmity

9. 1 Corinthians 2:11—it is aware of goods and benefits

10. Acts 18:15—it can be pressed

11. Acts 19:20—it can be purposed

[SESSION SEVEN - Cont.]

Leader: "How can couples tap into the spirit realm of a marriage? There are six different strategies:

1. Spend time in communion with God in personal prayer time

2. Spend time together in couple's devotion

3. Journal the leading of the Holy Spirit in your life

4. Become more sensitive to your feelings layered under your emotions

5. Write down the times when you had an intuition or premonition concerning your mate that was correct

6. Verify your intuitions that you have with your mate"

VI. COUPLES EXERCISE—REMEMBER THE TIME (20 MINUTES)

Leader: Have the couples turn to each other and discuss with each other a time when they had a feeling, intuition, or premonition about something concerning their partner that turned out to be true. Both partners should agree on the subject matter and then answer questions in their notebooks on this session. The following questions can be used to spark the discussions:

Have you ever sensed something about your spouse without them saying anything to you?

Have you ever picked up a vibe that something was going on with them?

Have you ever had a premonition or intuition about something that was about to happen?

VII. QUESTIONS AND ANSWERS (5 MINUTES)

Ask the couples if they have any questions about the discerning side of communication.

[SESSION SEVEN - Cont.]

VIII. HOMEWORK ASSIGNMENT (5 MINUTES)

Instruct the couples to spend each day trying to sense or feel certain things about their partners. Tell them to pray and ask God to make their spirits open to the leading of the Holy Spirit and sensitive to the spirits of their mate. Before the next meeting, couples are to sit down and discuss their perceptions with each other taking note of what was accurate or inaccurate. They are to fill in the information daily on the "Commune Sense" worksheet.

IX. CLOSURE (5 MINUTES)

Encourage a different couple at each meeting to give the closing prayer to include petitioning God's help for better discernment in communicating to each other.

"Dear Heavenly Father, we acknowledge You in all our ways and You direct our paths. We ask that You give us the spirit of revelation and discernment in our marriage by the power of the Holy Spirit. Help us to be sober and diligent because of our adversary, the devil. In Jesus' name, Amen."

X. FELLOWSHIP (15 MINUTES)

We encourage light, healthy snacks to top off the study.

[COMMUNE SENSE]

Date	Husband "I sensed my wife was…"	+	-	Wife "I sensed my husband was…"	+	-	Comments

+ means accurate
- means inaccurate

[SESSION EIGHT]

Leader's Guide for Session Eight—
Check Yourself

"By applying biblical principles, we were set free from our past hurts. This teaching helped to understand that God created us to fellowship with each other. It helped us to identify our personality types and how we communicate with each other. We took time to identify our problems and learned how to get victory over them. We will have disagreements, but we now have tools. These eight week sessions were a tremendous blessing for our marriage; they strengthened our love and commitment for each other."

— Alphonso and Dot

Goals for Session Eight:
- **To help couples understand male and female mental differences and how it can affect communication**
- **To understand the ten commandments of good communication**
- **To prepare couples for the process of confession and forgiveness**
- **To evaluate their progress and prepare for the monthly sessions**

Resources needed: FCLO Participant's Workbook for each person, Bibles for each couple, pens or pencils, and the FCLO DVD (eight week, session eight).

I. PRAYER (3 MINUTES)

Always begin with opening prayer.
Ask for prayer requests.

Prayer Module (optional)
    A—Adoration (Begin with praise for who God is)
    C—Confession (Time to admit sin and seek forgiveness from God)
    T—Thanksgiving (Giving appreciation to God for all He has done)
    S—Supplication (Making requests to God)

[SESSION EIGHT - Cont.]

II. WELCOME (2 MINUTES)

Introduce yourself and welcome all the couples who are attending. Make sure all couples have name tags.

III. HOMEWORK FEEDBACK (10 MINUTES)

Ask for a show of hands of couples who completed the homework from the last meeting. Have a few couples share their experience and what they learned from the homework. Continue to encourage the couples to do the homework as part of the learning process of communication.

IV. SHOW DVD (5 MINUTES)

Play the DVD introduction before the teaching session.

V. TEACHING (30 MINUTES)

*Have couples turn to session 8 to follow along and fill in the blanks as you read.

Leader: "In Genesis 1:27, we learn that 'God created people in his own image; God patterned them after himself; male and female he created them' (NLT). We are going to concentrate on the differences between males and females and how that affects the way they communicate.

"God created man and woman with differences in their brain make up. Scientists and psychologists have confirmed that the male and female brains aren't wired the same way and some of their differences affect how they communicate.

"For example, many wives can ask their husbands a question in the morning and don't get the answer until that evening. That is because he is processing the thought—there is more space between the hemispheres of his brain and it takes information longer to get from one side to the other.

"Because women can use both sides of their brains simultaneously—they can send mixed messages. When a husband asks his wife if she wants anything from the store and she responds with 'no,' but when he brings back snacks for himself—she wants to know if he brought her anything as well.

[SESSION EIGHT - Cont.]

"Men see the forest that is why it is difficult for them to find their razor on the cluttered table (they see everything) and women (with their detailed mind) see the tree and can filter through those objects quickly and help him find the razor.

"Although there are differences between the thought processes of the sexes, every couple can effectively communicate as they apply everything learned in the last eight weeks. Learning and living the Ten Commandments of Communication is a great start."

Instruct couples to turn to the Ten Commandments of Communication.

[SESSION EIGHT - Cont.]

Ten Commandments of Communication

I. Thou shalt talk to God before talking to others.
Psalm 19:14—Let the words of my mouth, and the meditation of my heart, be acceptable in thy sight, O LORD, my strength, and my redeemer. (KJV)

Leader: "It is important to talk to God first so that your words to your spouse will communicate life and bring healing, peace, information, and inspiration to them as you turn your mouth and mind over to God."

II. Thou shalt be swift to hear and slow to speak.
James 1:19—Understand [this], my beloved brethren. Let every man be quick to hear [a ready listener], slow to speak, slow to take offense and to get angry. (AMP)

Leader: "Couples should practice more listening and less speaking."

III. Thou shalt be clear, specific, and brief.
Matthew 5: 37—But let your communication be, yea, yea; nay, nay: for whatsoever is more than these cometh of evil. (KJV)

Leader: "Explain your terms, do not be vague and assume your partner understands or should 'just know' how you feel. Give short messages."

IV. Thou shalt stay in the here and now.
Philippians 3:13—Forgetting those things which are behind and reaching forth unto those things which are before. (KJV)

Leader: "Do not bring up old hurts and go through a list of old offenses; focus on the issue at hand."

V. Thou shalt look thy partner in the eye.
Matthew 6:22—The light of the body is the eye: if therefore thine eye be single, thy whole body shall be full of light. (KJV)

Leader: "Take the time to make eye contact. This tells your partner that you are listening and what they are saying is important to you."

[SESSION EIGHT - Cont.]

VI. Thou shalt not interrupt.
1 Peter 3:8—Finally, be ye all of one mind, having compassion one of another, love as brethren, be pitiful, be courteous (KJV)

Leader: "Do not interrupt your partner. You must be patient and listen, instead of just waiting for them to finish so you can make your point. That is why each of you should be brief and not give long sermons."

VII. Thou shalt do check back and echo.
Proverbs 15:23—A man hath joy by the answer of his mouth: and a word spoken in due season, how good is it! (KJV)

Leader: "Give a brief message and then check back to make sure your partner understood you. Ask a question like, 'What did you hear me say?' so they can repeat back the essence of what you said. You are not looking for a word for word response but an understanding of your general message. Confirm if your partner got the message. He or she will echo what you said and you will confirm if they are correct."

VIII. Thou shalt make "I" statements.
Psalm 39:3—I became very angry inside, and as I thought about it, my anger burned. So I spoke. (NCV)

Leader: "Speak for yourself, when you use the word 'you.' Often times you are blaming, i.e. 'You make me angry.' When you use the term 'we' you are not taking responsibility, i.e. 'We need to get our act together.' Instead say, 'I get angry when you do ____.'"

IV. Thou shalt make time to talk.
Ecclesiastes 3:7—There is…a time to keep silence, and a time to speak (KJV); the time for silence and the time for talk. (GNT)

Leader: "You need at least 15 minutes a day of uninterrupted, face-to-face communication. You may need more if there is an issue. Don't go to bed angry; you won't sleep well anyway. Take the time to talk before a bigger problem emerges."

[SESSION EIGHT - Cont.]

X. Thou shalt do the first nine commandments.
James 1:22 —But be ye doers of the word, and not hearers only, deceiving your own selves. (KJV)

Leader: "The wisdom of God won't help you if you don't walk in it and make a determination to put into practice what you have learned.

"Following the Ten Commandments of Communication will help improve communication between a husband and wife. However there will be hurt and pain, both intentional and unintentional. Healthy communication can bring healing to a fractured relationship. Following the simple process of confession can help."

Instruct couples to look at the Process of Confession.

Process of Confession

1) Acknowledge fault without denial.
2) Acknowledge the wrongness of the act.
3) Acknowledge the pain.
4) Give an apology.
5) Discuss any corrective action.
6) Be involved in the healing process.

For example:

"I was rude with you in front of your friends last week (1). I insulted you and cut you off (2). It was wrong, you were embarrassed, and it ruined the entire evening for you (3).

I'm sorry (4). I will call our friends, apologize for my behavior, and let them know that I have apologized to you as well (5). I will take you out for another evening to make up for it (6)."

[SESSION EIGHT - Cont.]

Leader: "Once your partner has confessed a sin, you must choose as an act of your will to forgive so that your spiritual growth won't be hindered. There is also a process of forgiveness as well.

"Forgiveness isn't about feelings but an act of your will. Make a choice to forgive and pray for your spouse when the enemy reminds you of the offense. Praying will change your heart and mind over time."

Process of Forgiveness

1) Choose as an act of your will to forgive.
2) Confess your hurt and anger with the offender.
3) Verbally state your forgiveness to the offender.
4) Discuss with the offender what corrective action is necessary.
5) Determine a positive act that you can do for the offender.

For example:

"I choose to forgive you (1) even though I was angry (2) about what you said to me. I forgive you (3). Apologizing for your behavior to our friends will be fine (#4), and you will know that I have forgiven you because I'll start speaking to you again (5)."

Leader: "Husbands aren't to become unforgiving and bitter with their wives or their prayers will be hindered. They are also to deal with their wives in knowledge and honor them as the weaker vessel according to Colossians 3:19 and 1 Peter 3:7.

"Wives must speak the truth in love and not try to embarrass or humiliate their husbands with words. According to Proverbs 12:4, 'a virtuous woman is a crown to her husband, but she that maketh ashamed is a rottenness in his bones.'"

[SESSION EIGHT - Cont.]

VI. COUPLES EXERCISE— (20 MINUTES)

Instruct the couples to go through two brief exercises (about 10 minutes each) to practice the Ten Commandments of Communication and the process of forgiveness.

A. Ten Commandments of Communication
Take a moment to review the commandments. Afterwards decide on one of your last disagreements and talk about it as a couple without breaking any of the Ten Commandments of Communication. Evaluate how well you followed the commandments and talk about the areas you both need to work on.

B. Confession Process
Husbands begin by choosing something they said or did recently that hurt your partner and go through each step of confession. Afterward, the wife should go through the forgiveness process. The wife then will pick something she said or did that was offensive, and the couple will go through the confession and forgiveness process.

VII. QUESTIONS AND ANSWERS (5 MINUTES)

Ask the couples if they have any questions about the chart, the Ten Commandments of Communication or the confession/forgiveness process.

VIII. PREPARATION FOR MONTHLY MEETINGS (5 MINUTES)

Leader: "Each couple involved in the communication study now has a great foundation to deal with issues that come up in their marriage. The next step of this study is to meet once a month to learn how to deal with issues that can trip up the most dedicated marriages. This is a great opportunity to continue developing good relationships and accountability with other couples while having fun and fellowship."

Have a sign up sheet available for couples wanting to meet monthly. Be sure to include pertinent information such as the date, time, and place.

IX. CLOSURE (5 MINUTES)

Encourage a different couple at each meeting to give the closing prayer to include petitioning God's help for better discernment in communicating to each other.

"Dear Heavenly Father, have Thine own way, Lord. You are the Potter and we are the clay. Make us and mold us according to Your will. Be the strength and peace on which we will stand. Reign in our home for You are worthy of glory. In Jesus' name, Amen."

X. FELLOWSHIP (15 MINUTES)

We encourage light, healthy snacks to top off the study.

[Ten Commandments of Communication]

I. _____

II. _____

III. _____

IV. _____

V. _____

VI. _____

VII. _____

VIII. _____

IX. _____

X. _____

[Process of Confession]

1) Acknowledge _____

2) Acknowledge _____

3) Acknowledge _____

4) Give _____

5) Discuss _____

6) Be _____

[Process of Forgiveness]

1) Choose _____

2) Confess _____

3) Verbally _____

4) Discuss _____

5) Determine _____

[References]

Merriam-Webster, I. *Merriam-Webster's Collegiate Dictionary.* 10th ed. Merriam-Webster: Springfield, Mass., 1996.

Strong, J. *The Exhaustive Concordance of the Bible,* electronic ed. Woodside Bible Fellowship: Ontario. 1996.

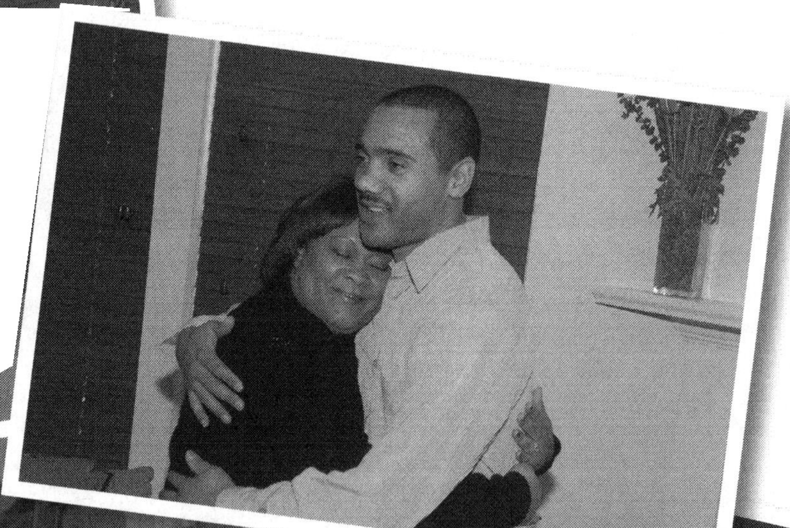

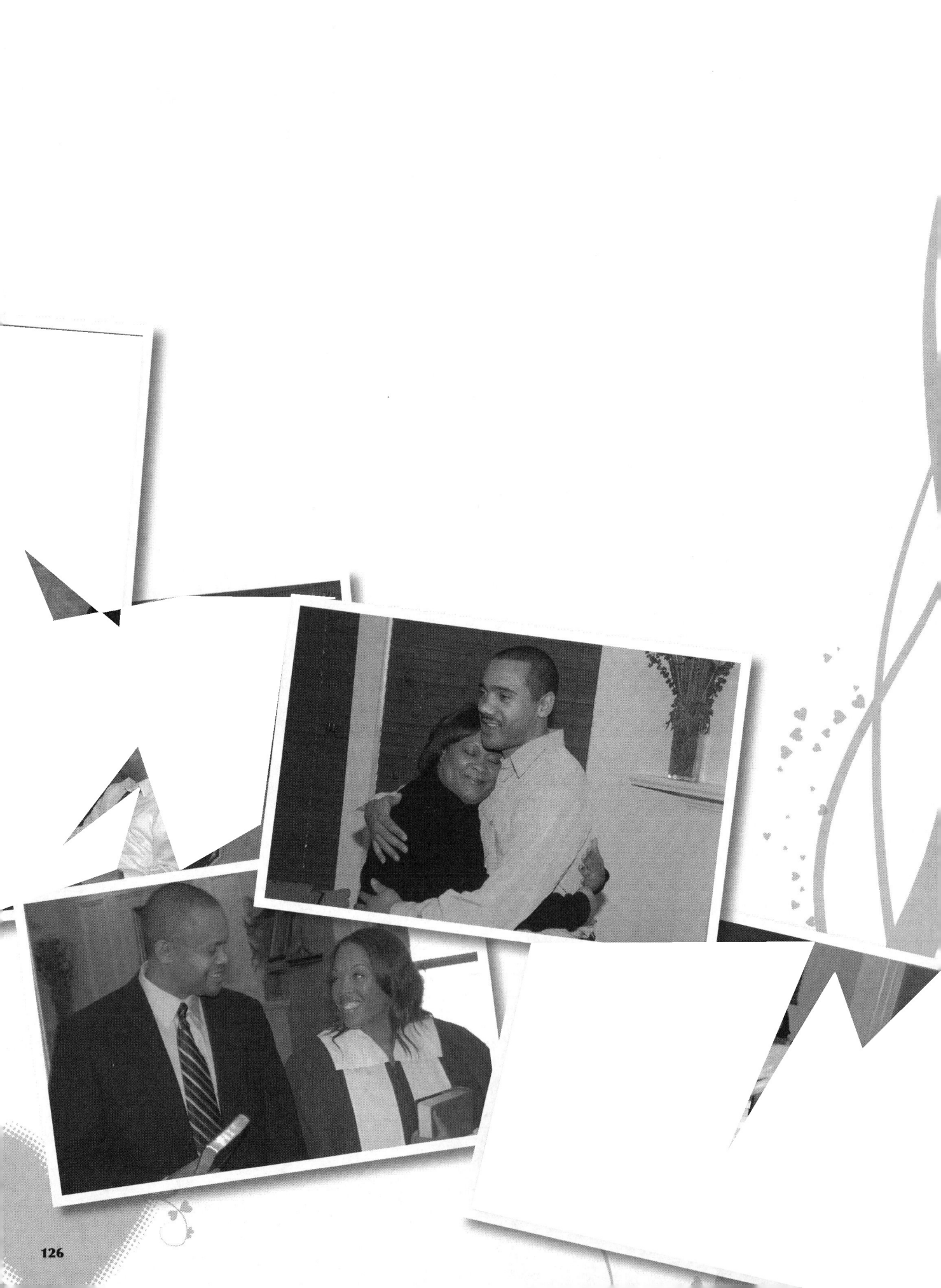

[FCLO MONTHLY ENRICHMENT PROGRAM]

Many waters cannot quench love,
Nor will rivers overflow it;
If a man were to give all the riches
of his house for love,
It would be utterly despised.

Song of Solomon 8:7, NIV

128

[A WORD FROM THE WALKERS]

We started a marriage enrichment group when we were engaged back in 1975. We pulled together couples who were also engaged and loved God. We all wanted to know God's plan for marriage. We met every month for many years going from house to house fellowshipping, sharing, studying the Word, and supporting each other. (Sounds like the early church.) As our children grew up together, other groups sprang up and spread though out our area. We loved one another, our marriages stayed strong, we talked about those things that bothered us and held each other accountable. We want you to know this wonderful experience.

We make no apologies for centering this curriculum on the Word of God, for we know that it is "quick and powerful and sharper than any two edged sword piercing and dividing asunder of soul and spirit." The Word of God will make us feel uncomfortable at times. The standard God sets goes against our sinful nature, and it is so high that we need His help. Yet God's way is the best way. We know it's tight, but it's right.

You are going to be sharing with friends every month and getting to know them in a new way. Each couple will have the opportunity to teach as the Holy Spirit flows through each of you to use your gifts to build each other up. We purposely don't give you the answers in the monthly curriculum for our main goal is for you to talk to your spouse, negotiate and set up the systems of your home. Remember, a good marriage takes a lifetime of learning.

Peace and Love

[HOW TO USE THIS MONTHLY MARRIAGE ENRICHMENT CURRICULUM]

1. Promote your upcoming couple enrichment program by using all available advertising venues. Your excitement about the training and communication course will be contagious to other couples as well. Recruit, confirm, and set up a place and time for your first session.

2. Each couple should take turns to lead the group in each session. As the lead couple, they will be the facilitators (not the teachers, trainers, or counselors). It works best if couples can take turns to host (provide refreshments) and lead the monthly session at their home. Each session has clear instructions about the preparation needed and the role of the leader. If a couple doesn't want to lead or host, arrangements should be in the group. Assign monthly sessions early on, or plan at the end of each session who will take the next meeting.

3. As the lead couple, husbands and wives need to determine the roles they will play for each session. For example, the husband can lead in the sharing and the wife can take the lead in the exercises. They can decide as a couple what works best for them. It would be beneficial to the group if the lead couple can work well together and model a fairly healthy relationship, remembering that, as an active couple in the group, you are learning and growing as well.

4. Consider couples who generally get along well together and have a few things in common. A minimum of three couples and a maximum of ten are suggested; with more than ten, it could get uncomfortable and crowded. It may be that one couple can accommodate the group and host every month. In this case, other couples can help with bringing in the refreshments. We recommend simple and healthy foods.

    a. You can have meetings in other settings like a church, but we encourage the comfort level in a home.

    b. Determine a visitor policy ahead of time. Visitors are not recommended because private information may be shared between the couples.

    c. If the group is connected to the church ministry, your pastor may require that all the participants be members of the church. Or they may want the group used more as outreach and allow non-members to participate. Check with the pastor for direction.

    d. Encourage your group to set up and become settled with in the first two months. Avoid too many disruptions of coming and going that will damage the feeling of trust and comfort to share.

5. Use the first meeting for fellowship and fun so that couples will get to know each other. Couples can cover the basic format and give input about what day of the week and month is best for them. Couples need to commit to a year and purchase their workbooks.

6. Emphasize confidentiality so that things shared in the group won't be shared with others. You may want everyone to sign a confidentiality covenant; this is not a legal document but a covenant before God.

7. Every couple needs to have contact information (email, home, cell, or work numbers) of each member of the group for cancellations, emergencies, or other group communications.

8. Close the first session with prayer, refreshments and games (such as Charades).

9. Couples will need a private, quiet, clean, and comfortable setting where people are not cramped for space. Make a decision on how to handle childcare.

10. It is best for husband and wife to attend together, but there may be circumstances that keep one partner from being able to attend. (However, it shouldn't be a regular pattern.)

11. Be careful to keep the atmosphere pleasant and positive. Refer couples to pastors, professional counselors, police, or doctors when needed.

12. These sessions are not counseling or deliverance sessions. They are to enrich the couples with an opportunity to share and care for one another, deal with issues, understand the Word of God, pray, encourage, and be accountable to each other.

13. Participating couples should have fun and fellowship with each other outside of the monthly sessions to build strong relationships.

14. Keep in mind some sessions may take longer than one session, especially when you discuss points that really stir up deeper issues. Feel free to continue the next month if the group is in agreement and needs to discuss more.

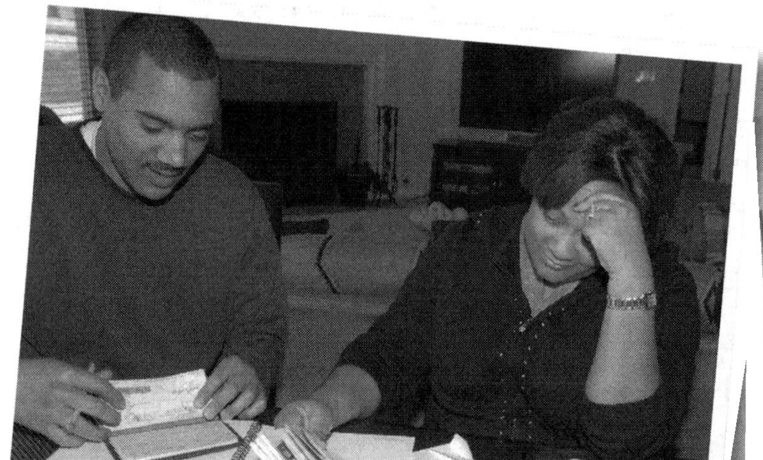

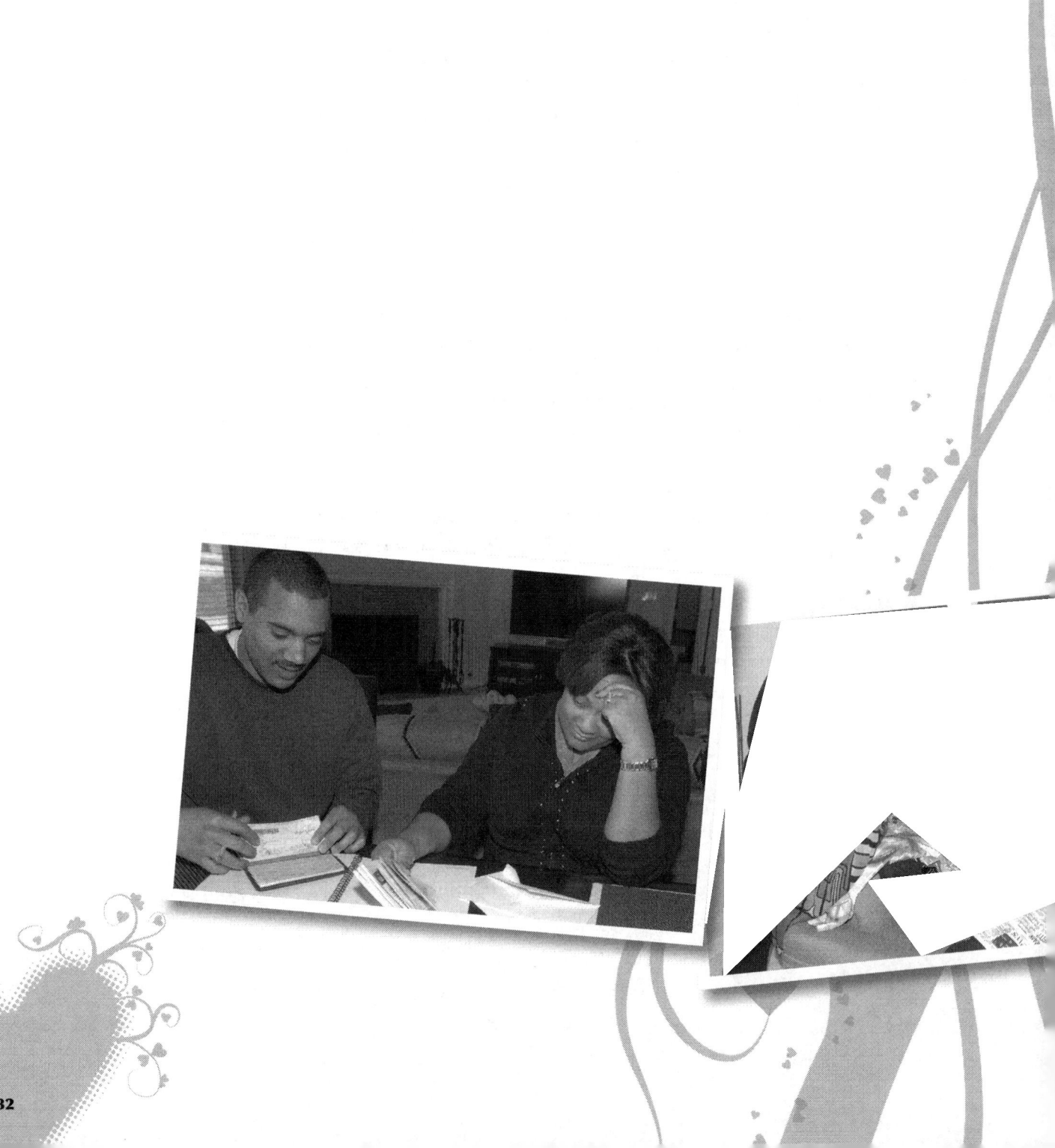

[SESSION ONE]
TALKING MONEY WITH YOUR HONEY

From Ja'Ola Walker:

"When we first married, Pastor Clarence paid all the bills. Since I really didn't pay attention to what we had or didn't have, I picked up what I wanted. One day he said, 'Let's sit down and do the bills together.'

After we finished, I came to the revelation that we didn't have money for me to spend unwisely. So my mother taught me to live more tightly. My husband then decided to delegate the bills to me. I handle all the money and have full access to it. I love a good sale, and my husband doesn't have to worry about the credit card being maxed out and not having enough money to pay the mortgage. Tithing is very important to us. We have had times when neither of us were working and because we continued to tithe every bill was paid. God is faithful. This is a wonderful promise we can hold on to in these hard economic times."

Goals for Session One:
- **Glorify God and bring Him honor in good stewardship of finances**
- **Help couples better understand the role of finances in their conflicts**
- **Reduce conflicts in marriages about finances**
- **Educate couples on increasing income and decreasing debt**

[SESSION ONE]
TALKING MONEY WITH YOUR HONEY - Cont.

Lead Couple: *Greet couples warmly, begin with opening song, take prayer requests, and lead the couples in an opening prayer.*

Prayer Requests:

_____

_____

_____

Lead Couple: *Assign Scriptures to couples to read out loud before starting the DVD.*

SCRIPTURE READING FOR SESSION ONE

Proverbs 24:3–4
"By wisdom a house is built, and through understanding it is established; through knowledge its rooms are filled with rare and beautiful treasures."

Ecclesiastes 5:19–20
"Moreover, when God gives any man health and possessions, and enables him to enjoy them, to accept his lot and be happy in his work—this is a gift of God. He seldom reflects on the days of his life, because God keeps him occupied with gladness of heart."

Psalms 112:1–3
"Praise the Lord. Blessed is the man who fears the Lord, who finds great delight in his commands. His children will be mighty in the land; the generation of the upright will be blessed. Wealth and riches are in his house, and his righteousness endures forever."

Lead Couple: *Play DVD for "Talking Money with your Honey" and lead a discussion based on the following questions:*

Have you ever encountered conflicts about money in your marriage? How did you handle it?

[SESSION ONE]
TALKING MONEY WITH YOUR HONEY - Cont.

SHARING SEGMENT

Lead Couple: *"Money is the source of many couple's fights and arguments. The lack of money can place great hardship and stress on couple relations that result in tension, abuse, and sometimes separation and divorce."*

"Why does money cause so much conflict in marriage?"

_____

_____

_____

_____

Other reasons:

- Unresolved problems of self-esteem issues
- Unresolved power and control issues
- Fear that the love has left the marriage
- Each spouse often follows their own family legacy, loyalties, and values about money
- Different gender perspectives about money.
- Lack of money
- Resisting the biblical principles regarding money

[SESSION ONE]
TALKING MONEY WITH YOUR HONEY - Cont.

Lead Couple: *"The following ten principles give real solutions to the most common money conflicts between couples.*

1) Get an understanding about the root causes of your money conflicts.

2) Confess to your spouse your responsibility in creating the financial problems.

3) Identify your family's influence or legacy that may still have a hold on your finances.

4) Develop an attitude of contentment about money.

5) Communicate your feelings about money, and respect your partner's view even if it is different from yours.

6) Spouses should negotiate together on a practical budget and stay with it by going over finances with an awareness of assets and debt. Decide who will pay the bills and what accounts are used.

7) Deal with one financial chore at a time. Don't try to establish a budget and investment decisions all at once.

8) Recognize the value of the unpaid work of a spouse who chooses to stay at home.

9) Make sure each partner has money to spend without having to consult the other.

[SESSION ONE]
TALKING MONEY WITH YOUR HONEY - Cont.

Lead Couple: *"What are some biblical principles to help couples decrease debt and increase their assets?"*

Pay your _____
(Malachi 3:7–12)

We live by _____
(2 Corinthians 5:7)

Do not withhold _____
(Proverbs 3:27)

Let no debt _____
(Romans 13:8)

Lazy hands make _____
(Proverbs 10:4)

A good man _____
(Proverbs 13:22)

He who puts up _____
(Proverbs 11:15)

Be sure you know _____
(Proverbs 27:23)

Sit down and first _____
(Luke 14:28)

The plans of the diligent _____
(Proverbs 21:5)

Each man should give _____
(2 Corinthians 9:7)

[SESSION ONE]
TALKING MONEY WITH YOUR HONEY - Cont.

Lead Couple: *Instruct couples to take ten minutes to complete section A and B of the financial attitude questionnaire separately and come together to compare answers. After ten minutes have passed, begin a group discussion using the following questions as guidelines.*

Complete the Financial Attitudes Questionnaire.

What role has money played in any of your marital conflicts?

What money messages did you bring into marriage, and how have they contributed to money fights?

What other underlying issues could spark money battles?

Which of the Ten Principles for Resolving Conflict or Ten Biblical Principles can be immediately incorporated in your handling of money? Which ones are perceived to be more difficult? Why?

Lead Couple: *Read over home assignment and encourage couples to complete it by the next meeting date.*

Home Assignment:

Communicate and negotiate your financial affairs by:
- **Developing a budget using the Financial Attitude Questionnaire**
- **Determine your financial goals and your plan for achieving it**

Lead Couple: *Close out session one with a song and prayer. Encourage couples to pray together daily. End with a time of refreshments and fellowship.*

[FINANCIAL ATTITUDE QUESTIONNAIRE]

A. Feelings about Money

Check all appropriate answers:

1. Independent _____
    Secure   _____
    Successful   _____
    Loved   _____
    Powerful   _____

    All of the above   _____
    None of the above _____

    Other _____
    _____

2. Explain how you feel when you spend money on yourself.
    _____
    _____
    _____

3. Explain how you feel when you spend money on others.
    _____
    _____

4. How would you feel if you had more money or spending freedom?
    _____
    _____
    _____

[FINANCIAL ATTITUDE QUESTIONNAIRE]

B.   Determine if your arguments are about money

1. Do you feel that you are having the same arguments about money?

    Yes _____   No _____

2. Are you more upset about the reasoning behind spending the money more than the amount of money spent?

    Yes _____   No _____

3. Are either or both of you talking with more emotion on the subject than it requires?

    Yes _____   No _____

4. Have your emotions been the same even if the fights have been about different things?

    Yes _____   No _____

[Basic Household Budget]

Year $_____   Month $_____   Available Income for the Month $_____

Monthly Payment Items	Currently Spending	Goal Spending	New Monthly Budget
1. Tithe			
2. Tax			
3. Housing			
4. Savings			
5. Insurance			
6. Food			
7. Debts			
8. Medical			
9. Child Care			
10. Clothing			
11. Investments			
12. Recreation			
13. Miscellaneous			
14. Miscellaneous			
15. Miscellaneous			
Total for Items 3–15			
Leftover Income			

[Our Financial Plan]

Our Goal	Our Priority	Method for Achieving	Biblical Principle or Promise

[SESSION TWO]
CLOSE ENCOUNTERS OF THE LOVE KIND

From Ja'Ola Walker:

"I'm a woman who likes affection and emotional intimacy, but my precious husband grew up learning to be a loner, and he is good at shutting folk out when he wants. The Lord taught him about the importance of my emotions and his responsibility to communicate with me early in our marriage as he studied the Word. So now, the only time he gives me the emotional freeze is when he is angry. I used to go through all kinds of guilt and distress, but I learned to evaluate my behavior, apologize about my part of the problem, and not take responsibility for his issue. I allow him to be angry, give him his space, and I keep going. He will soon come out of it, apologize, and together we move on."

Goals for Session Two:
- **Glorify God and bring honor to Him in couple proximity**
- **Help couples better understand the importance of closeness and independence**
- **Enable couples to develop appropriate amount of closeness and space**

Lead Couple: *Greet couples warmly, begin with opening song, take prayer requests, and lead the couples in an opening prayer.*

Prayer Requests:

_____

_____

_____

Lead Couple: *Assign Scriptures to couples to read out loud before starting the DVD.*

[SESSION TWO]
CLOSE ENCOUNTERS OF THE LOVE KIND - Cont.

Scripture Reading for Session Two

Genesis 2:20–25
"So the man gave names to all the livestock, the birds of the air and all the beasts of the field. But for Adam no suitable helper was found.

So the Lord God caused the man to fall into a deep sleep and while he was sleeping, he took one of the man's ribs and closed up the place with flesh.

Then the Lord God made a woman from the rib he had taken out of the man, and he brought her to the man.

The man said, 'This is now bone of my bones and flesh of my flesh; she shall be called "woman," for she was taken out of man.'

For this reason a man will leave his father and mother and be united to his wife, and they will become one flesh.

The man and his wife were both naked, and they felt no shame."

Ephesians 5:31
"For this cause shall a man leave his father and mother, and shall be joined unto his wife, and they two shall be one flesh."

Lead Couple: Play DVD for "Close Encounters of the Love Kind" and lead a discussion based on the following questions:

- Is it OK for a spouse to spend time away from home with their friends?
- How much is too much time away from your spouse?
- Are the exceptions for co-workers, family, or old friends?

[SESSION TWO]
CLOSE ENCOUNTERS OF THE LOVE KIND - Cont.

Sharing Segment:

Lead Couple: *"Couples must find the right mixture of closeness and space in marriage. Too much closeness in marriage leads to emotionally smothering each other. Too much space in marriage leads to living like strangers."*

Yet Ephesians 5:31 gives the command that husbands and wives are to cleave to each other. For men, the Hebrew word for "cleave" found in Genesis 2:24 is *dabaq* (daw-bak) which means to catch by pursuit, to follow hard after or to glue oneself to closely.

What does this mean for husbands?
- Intimacy must be pursued and pursued hard; it's not automatic.
- Intimacy and closeness are goals to be pursued.
- The pursuit of intimacy and closeness are to be ongoing even after marriage.

For women, the Hebrew word for "desire" in Genesis 3:16 is *teshuwqah* (tesh-oo-kaw) which means a longing after, a stretching out after, or running after. It is different from the male as it is more feeling oriented rather than action oriented.

What does this mean for wives?
- Her desire and craving is for her own husband.
- She will welcome her husband's affection.
- She will be drawn to her husband.

[SESSION TWO]
CLOSE ENCOUNTERS OF THE LOVE KIND - Cont.

The following chart reveals the difference between the male and female in cleaving:

Dabaq	Teshuwqah
Male	Female
- Pursuing; follow after; catch	- Longing after; running after and running over
- Behavioral action oriented	- Emotional feeling oriented
- Pre-fall objective (before Adam fell into sin, this was God's desire for him)	- Post-fall corrective (after Eve fell into sin, this became God's way to correct her)
- Single message: pursue after, catch, stick	- Double message: to run after and run over

The Greek word for "joined" in Ephesians 5:31 is *proskollao* (pros-kol-lah-o) which means "to glue to; to adhere to; to glue upon; to join oneself to closely." What are some ways that husbands and wives avoid closeness with each other?

_____

_____

_____

_____

Other examples:

Husbands
Shut down communication
Avoids physical contact
Over-involvement in work or ministry
Excessive time spent with friends
Creating arguments, puts wife down
Physical abuse
Substance abuse
Extramarital affairs

Wives
Denies sexual relations, avoids touching
Too much involvement with children
Attempts to dominate or control husband
Being argumentative or critical
Over-involvement with parents
Shutting down communication
Excessive time on phone with friends
Over-involvement with activities outside of home

[SESSION TWO]
CLOSE ENCOUNTERS OF THE LOVE KIND - Cont.

Lead Couple: *"Here are ten suggestions to initiate and pursue closeness as a couple. Give at least one specific example of how couples can make each suggestion work in their marriage."*

1) Commit to being close to God and obeying His Word
   Example: _____

2) Deal with any unfinished business with parents
   Example: _____

3) Acknowledge any underlying fears
   Example: _____

4) Learn how to laugh, be silly, and give a lot of little surprises
   Example: _____

5) Reduce negative criticism and increase positive compliments
   Example: _____

6) Get away together as often as you can
   Example: _____

7) Maintain a passionate sex life
   Example: _____

8) Find a vision and purpose you can work on together
   Example: _____

9) Identify Satan's method of attack on your marriage and purpose to fight against him together
   Example: _____

10) Make praying together a priority
    Example: _____

[SESSION TWO]
CLOSE ENCOUNTERS OF THE LOVE KIND - Cont.

Lead Couple: *Read the following exercise to the couples and have a discussion using the questions following it.*

Sit in a chair facing your spouse with your knees about six inches apart. Outstretch your arms and match your palms with your spouse. Try to move closer to your spouse with your arms still extended. Afterward, gradually bend your elbows allowing shorter distances between you. Keep bending and getting closer to each other. Reverse the process, straightening your arms gradually back to outstretched position, but still try to get closer.

What is your experience with closeness and distance issues?

What ways have your past family experiences affected your closeness in marriage?

Lead Couple: *"As long as your hands were outstretched in a rigid and unbending position, it was difficult to be close. The more you bent your elbows, the closer you were able to move to each other. Sometimes, in order to be closer, you must learn how to be flexible and bend."*

Lead Couple: *Read over the home assignment and encourage couples to complete it by the next meeting date.*

[SESSION TWO]
CLOSE ENCOUNTERS OF THE LOVE KIND - Cont.

Home Assignment:

Sit facing each other and come up with the top three moments when you both felt very close. Share details about each of them together. For example, where and when did they occur? What happened previously and afterward? What did you like about each other during those times? What did you do to feel close to each other?

Complete the Closeness/Distance Enablement Sheet individually and come together to share your results.

Lead Couple: *Close out this session with a song and prayer. Encourage couples to pray together daily. End with a time of refreshments and fellowship.*

[CLOSENESS/DISTANCE ENABLEMENT SHEET]

I need to be close with my partner in the following:

Need: For example: I need my husband to hold me before he gets up or turns over.	Frequency: For example: For at least ten minutes every time after we have sex.
1.	1.
2.	2.
3.	3.
4.	4.
5.	5.

I need space from my partner in the following:

Need: For example: I need my wife to give me space to hang out with my friends.	Frequency: For example: For the entirety of a Saturday football game.
1.	1.
2.	2.
3.	3.
4.	4.
5.	5.

We agree to be close in the following:

Reason: For example: We can have dinner together, talk about the message, and pray together.	Frequency: For example: Every Sunday after church
1.	1.
2.	2.
3.	3.
4.	4.
5.	5.

152

[SESSION THREE]
LABOR OF LOVE

From Pastor Clarence:

"I know every woman is different, but Ja'Ola was created by God to balance me out. We have learned to work together as a team. We naturally flow into certain jobs based on our strengths. Sometimes we do things based on the situation; when my wife isn't at home, I handle everything. I do the shopping and I take care of my clothes on a regular basis. We have a busy schedule so if I want to cook something special; I buy it and prepare it. It's not a big deal. Jesus was a man's man; He cooked a fish dinner for His disciples."

Goals for Session Three:
- **Glorify God and bring Him honor with the labor in the home**
- **Enable couples to better understand the role of issues regarding household responsibility in marital conflict**
- **Help couples negotiate a better division of labor in the home and reduce conflicts about household responsibilities**

Lead Couple: *Greet couples warmly, begin with opening song, take prayer requests, and lead the couples in an opening prayer.*

Prayer Requests:

_____

_____

_____

[SESSION THREE]
LABOR OF LOVE - Cont.

Lead Couple: *Assign Scriptures to couples to read out loud together before starting the DVD.*

Scripture Reading for Session Three

Titus 2:4–5
"Then they can teach the younger women to love their husbands and children, to be self-controlled and pure, to be busy at home, to be kind, and to be subject their husbands so that no one will malign the word of God."

1 Timothy 5:8
"If anyone does not provide for his relatives, and especially for his immediate family, he has denied the faith and is worse than an unbeliever."

Ecclesiastes 4:9
"Two are better than one, because they have a good return for their work."

Lead Couple: *Play DVD for "Labor of Love" and lead a discussion based on the following questions:*

What do you think?

How do you divide the responsibilities in your home?
How do the roles you play differ in comparison to those of your parents?

[SESSION THREE]
LABOR OF LOVE - Cont.

Sharing Segment:

Lead Couple: *"Different expectations regarding how housework is divided can lead to arguments and conflict."*

What does the Bible reveal about husbands and the home according to:

1 Timothy 5:8 _____

Ecclesiastes 10:18 _____

Proverbs 24:30–32 _____

List specific ways that husbands can fulfill their duties for the home based on the Scriptures above:

1. _____

2. _____

3. _____

In 1 Timothy 5:8, the Greek word for provide is *prongeo* (pron-o-eh-o) which means to consider in advance, to look out for beforehand, to take thought in advance, or to foresee the need. How can wives encourage their husbands in their God-given abilities?

_____

_____

Provision in the Bible amounted to three things: money, goods, and services. Home responsibilities falls in the service category. The first job Adam received from God was taking care of his home—making Adam the first homemaker.

[SESSION THREE]
LABOR OF LOVE - Cont.

Lead Couple: *What does the Bible reveal about women and the home in the following verses?*

Titus 2:5 _____

Proverbs 31:10–31 _____
_____
_____

List the specific ways that wives can fulfill their duties in the home based on the Scriptures above:

_____
_____
_____

The Greek word for "keepers" is *oikourose* (oy-koo-roos) which means a guard, a watcher, a stay-at-home who is domestically inclined, a good housekeeper, or a "worker at home."

What can husbands do to encourage wives in their role of taking care of the home?

_____
_____
_____

Lead Couple: *The Bible clearly communicates the responsibility of the wife as the keeper of the home. A woman can be encouraged to focus on these seven steps towards accomplishing her God-given position.*

1) Think of her home as a place where God dwells
2) Open her home as a place of hospitality
3) Remember the physical home is a reflection of what is in her mind
4) Overcome resistance and family issues in regards to housework
5) Understand how it will contribute to marital harmony
6) Recognize and deal with Satan's attack on the family
7) Use housework as an opportunity to exercise and take care of herself

Are these seven steps realistic? Why or why not?

_____

_____

_____

How can the following Scriptures help a wife who feels overwhelmed with her role as keeper of the home?

Psalm 55:22 _____

Isaiah 46:4 _____

[SESSION THREE]
LABOR OF LOVE

Lead Couple: *Direct the group's attention to the chart below.*

This chart shows general strengths and tendencies; of course there are men who love to cook and women who are better at electrical repairs. It doesn't matter what side of the list you are on; just begin to think about your strengths and how you can contribute to your home.

Lead a discussion with the questions below.

[Table of the Characteristics Common for Men and Women]

MEN	WOMEN
Unity of mind, narrowness of vision Potential job: Plumbing/carpentry	Better at understanding complexities Potential job: Organizing
More muscle tissue, more upper body strength Potential job: Heavy lifting	Less muscle tone; more strength waist down Potential job: Light lifting
Programmed to move toward one direction Potential job: Mowing/mopping	Can see things from many angles Potential job: Grocery shopping
Better at linear reasoning Potential job: Electrical repairs	Superior in use of all five senses Potential job: Cooking/sewing
Less sensitive to loud noises; more sensitive to bright lights Potential job: Hammering/drilling	More sensitive to loud noises; less sensitive to bright lights Potential job: Washing, sweeping
More color-blind Potential job: Implementing her design	Less color-blind Potential job: Home décor
Three-dimensional abilities Potential job: Building projects	Better at remembering location of items Potential job: Organizing

[SESSION THREE]
LABOR OF LOVE

What household responsibilities cause the most conflict in your marriage?
What might be some of the underlying causes?
How were these responsibilities handled in your childhood home?
How might this influence your attitude about household duties?

Lead Couple: *Read over home assignment and encourage couples to complete it by the next meeting date.*

Home Assignment:
Complete the Chore Responsibility worksheet.

Lead Couple: *Scripture doesn't dictate who does the dishes or fixes the plumbing. The key is for the two of you to come up with a system that you can both live with. Pray, talk, negotiate, and use all of your options—children, a dishwasher, a cleaning service—as long as it gets done. Think as a team and work together to make and keep a lovely home.*

Lead Couple: *Close out this session with a song and prayer. Encourage couples to pray together daily. End with a time of refreshments and fellowship.*

[Chore Responsibility Worksheet]

Chore	Husband Only	Wife Only	Primary Wife, Husband Helps	Primary Husband, Wife Helps	Jointly

[SESSION FOUR]
MARRIED WITH CHILDREN

From the Walkers:

"Our children have blessed and challenged our marriage. They have had their share of problems that pulled on our marriage and pushed us to our knees. We are stronger prayer warriors because of them. Through our children, our faith has grown, we know God on a different level, and we are more empathetic towards other parents. Both our sons are bright, talented, and loving young adults who have accepted the Lord. We still pray that God will fulfill His plan for their lives."

Goals for Session Four:
- To glorify God and bring honor to His name
- To better understand the impact of children on marriage and vice versa
- To enable couples to deal with the challenges of balancing marriage and children

Lead Couple: *Greet couples warmly, begin with opening song, take prayer requests, and lead the couples in an opening prayer.*

Prayer Requests:

_____

_____

_____

[SESSION FOUR]
MARRIED WITH CHILDREN - Cont.

Lead Couple: *Assign Scriptures to couples to read out loud before starting the DVD.*

Scripture Reading for Session Four

Genesis 1:28
"God blessed them and said to them, 'Be fruitful and increase in number; fill the earth and subdue it.'"

1 Corinthians 14:20
"Brothers, stop thinking like children. In regard to evil be infants, but in your thinking be adults."

Psalm 127:3–5
"Sons are a heritage from the Lord, children a reward from him. Like arrows in the hands of a warrior are sons born in one's youth. Blessed is the man whose quiver is full of them. They will not be put to shame when they contend with their enemies in the gate."

Lead Couple: *Play DVD for "Married with Children" and lead a discussion based on the following questions:*

What do you think?

What happens when parents don't agree on child-rearing issues?
How can parents be in one accord on child rearing?

[SESSION FOUR]
MARRIED WITH CHILDREN - Cont.

Sharing Segment

Lead Couple: *"Children are a gift from God and can enhance a marriage. They can also be a source of conflict in marriage as the role of a parent can sometimes be in contradiction of the role of a spouse."*

What do the following Scriptures teach us about children in marriage?

Genesis 1:28 _____

_____

Psalm 127:3–5 _____

_____

_____

Parents are the tree and children are the fruit who give strength and life to the cycle of the family tree. Parents are to take care of their children. They are a means by which families are to excel, gain authority, and take dominion. Parents are to fill the earth with God-images through their children. Children help a couple to extend the rule of God on the earth, and they are a legacy from God.

[SESSION FOUR]
MARRIED WITH CHILDREN - Cont.

What are some ways that children can positively impact a marriage?

_____

_____

_____

_____

Other ideas:
- Enhance the love already in the marriage
- Reduce tension as they can divert a couple's focus from problems
- Keep couples married
- Teach parents how to give unconditional love
- Helps parents realize and change negative patterns passed on by other generations
- Encourages parents to enjoy life and have fun
- Brings an opportunity to leave a godly heritage
- Strengthens the unity bond between couples in times of joy and sorrow

What are some ways that couples can experience discord over children?

_____

_____

_____

_____

Other ideas:
- Infertility problems, disagreement about the time to have children or whether to have children at all
- Spouse gives children more attention than to their partner
- Parental duties can reduce time for sexual intimacy and time alone
- Disagreement between couples on discipline issues
- Stress from lack of finances
- Unplanned arrival of children
- Parents forming coalitions with children against a spouse

[SESSION FOUR]
MARRIED WITH CHILDREN - Cont.

Rebellious, disobedient, or prodigal children can put stress on a marriage. Couples have to keep their focus on strengthening their marriage through difficult days of child-rearing.

Lead Couple: *"Does your marriage positively or negatively affect your children? How?"*

_____

_____

_____

_____

Points to ponder:
- Your marriage provides the behavior and interaction your children will replicate when they get married.
- Your marriage influences the choices they will make for a spouse.
- Your marital conflicts can affect your children's school performance, cause them to get involved with it, or cause them to develop behavioral or health problems as a distraction from your fighting.

[SESSION FOUR]
MARRIED WITH CHILDREN - Cont.

Lead Couple: *The following points can help parents leave a positive marital legacy to their children and reduce the amount of conflicts surrounding them.*

1) Put your marriage before the children (Genesis 2:24).

2) Refrain from involving children in marital conflicts.

3) Make time for each other (Ecclesiastes 3:1).

4) Resist living your life through your children

5) Pray, discuss, and negotiate the timing of having children (Proverbs 3:5,6; 24:27).

6) Have a budget which includes saving money for your children and grandchildren (Proverbs 13:22; 24:27).

7) Raise children according to God's original purpose of being fruitful, multiplying, and replenishing a godly heritage (Genesis 1:28, Psalm 27:3).

8) Agree on a consistent disciplinary plan when dealing with disobedience (Amos 3:3, Proverbs 22:6).

Lead Couple: *Begin a group discussion with the following questions:*

How have your children positively or negatively affected your marriage? (Please answer from your perspective: blended families, young children, teens or adult children.)

What can you change to make the negatives a positive in your marriage?

[SESSION FOUR]
MARRIED WITH CHILDREN - Cont.

Lead Couple: *Read over home assignment and encourage couples to complete it by the next meeting date.*

Home Assignment:

Complete the Parent/Child Re-Alignment Sheet

Lead Couple: *Close out this session with a song and prayer. Encourage couples to pray together daily. End with a time of refreshments and fellowship.*

[PARENT/CHILD RE-ALIGNMENT SHEET]

BEFORE Unhealthy Conditions	AFTER New Arrangement
Ways Our Children Come Between Us	**Our New Arrangement**
Time Demands With Children	**New Arrangement**

[SESSION FIVE]
JUST A FRIENDLY MATTER

From the Walkers:

"We asked the Lord to lead us to friends who would get along well with both of us. Sometimes it's not so easy. Both husbands and wives have to all like each other. We went on a vacation with a couple who were very competitive, even down to comparing children. It was very hard to relax with them. Over the years we have accumulated a few good couple friends, and we cherish our time with them. They are the type of people we can dream with, seek encouragement, and be supportive. We can be ourselves since they don't have agendas; they aren't competing with us, nor do they feel threatened by us."

Goals for Session Five:
- **To glorify God and bring honor to His name**
- **To enable couples to better understand the role of friends in a conflict**
- **To help couples develop the proper relations with friends outside a marriage**

Lead Couple: *Greet couples warmly, begin with opening song, take prayer requests, and lead the couples in an opening prayer.*

Prayer Requests:

_____

_____

_____

Lead Couple: *Assign Scriptures for couples to read out loud before starting the DVD.*

[SESSION FIVE]
JUST A FRIENDLY MATTER - Cont.

Scripture Reading for Session Five

Proverbs 18:24
"A man of many companions may come to ruin, but there is a friend who sticks closer than a brother."

Proverbs 17:17
"A friend loves at all times, and a brother is born for adversity."

Proverbs 27:6
"Wounds from a friend can be trusted, but an enemy multiplies kisses."

John 15:13
"Greater love has no one than this, that he lay down his life for his friends."

Lead Couple: *Play DVD for "Just a Friendly Matter" and lead a discussion based on the following questions:*

What do you think?

How much time is too much time for your spouse to spend with friends?
Is it okay for married people to have single friends?
Should married people have friends of the opposite sex?

Sharing Segment

Lead Couple: *"Friends can be a tremendous blessing to a marriage as a great source of strength, encouragement, and accountability. Each couple must learn to deal with issues that may arise out of friendships."*

Do friendships change after marriage? Why or why not?

_____

_____

_____

[SESSION FIVE]
JUST A FRIENDLY MATTER

Very close friendships before marriage can change because the couple replaces a best friend with a spouse who is the object of intimacy. Men and women view friendships differently: women are more relationship oriented (more intimate) and men's friendships are more centered around work and complementing interests.

How can friendships enhance a marital relationship?

_____

_____

_____

Other examples:
- Friends can fill gaps that marital relations leave open (e.g. women can get emotional connection from another woman, men can get physical competition from other men).
- Friends can provide positive marital role models.

How can friendships cause conflict and division in a marriage?

_____

_____

_____

Other examples:
- A spouse spends more time and communication with a friend than they do with their partner (creates jealousy).
- A friend can have a negative influence on a spouse.
- A friend can become over-involved in the couples conflict and form a coalition with one spouse
- A friend can become an extramarital lover.

[SESSION FIVE]
JUST A FRIENDLY MATTER - Cont.

Lead Couple: *"How do the following Scriptures reveal how friendships can enhance a marriage?"*

Prioritize and limit your friends.
(Proverbs 18:24) _____

Determine the boundaries of the friendships.
(Proverbs 4:7) _____

Resist making promises or agreements with friends before confirming with spouse.
(Amos 3:3) _____

Don't entertain friends who are negative about your spouse, flirtatious with your spouse, or have conflicts with your spouse.
(Proverbs 16:28) _____

Choose a couple who gets along well with the both of you and can be good travel companions.
(Psalm 133:1) _____

Opposite-sex relationships should be limited to time together as a couple or with family to guard against sexual temptations.
(Proverbs 5:15-20) _____

Lead Couple: *Lead a discussion using the following questions:*

How have friends challenged our marriage?

What are the warning signs of when a friendship is beginning to hurt a marriage?

What boundaries do couples need to create to protect their marriage?

If a spouse doesn't agree with their partner's selection of friends, how should they deal with it?

Lead Couple: Instruct each couple to fill out the answers separately and come together to share their answers.

[SESSION FIVE]
JUST A FRIENDLY MATTER - Cont.

A Friend Indeed

1. My spouse's best friends are:
   _____

2. Our funniest friends:
   _____

3. Friends living in other places:
   _____

4. What I like most about my partner's friends:
   _____

5. We are developing new friendships with:
   _____

Lead Couple: *Read over home assignment and encourage couples to complete it by the next meeting date.*

Home Assignment:

Complete the "It's A Friendly Matter" worksheet.

Lead Couple: *Close out this session with a song and prayer. Encourage couples to pray together daily. End with a time of refreshments and fellowship.*

[IT'S A FRIENDLY MATTER WORKSHEET]

The friends we would like to spend more time with are:

We will spend time with _____ on a _____ basis.

They will be involved in our lives in the following ways:
_____
_____

They will not be involved in the following ways:
_____
_____

We will be involved in their lives in the following ways:
_____
_____

We will not be involved in their lives in the following ways:
_____
_____

The friends we will limit our time and involvement with are:
_____
_____

We will only be involved in the following ways:

_____

_____

We will not be involved in the following ways:

_____

_____

Husband's top five expectations for his wife's friendships:

a._____

b._____

c._____

d._____

e._____

Wife's top five expectations for husband's friendships:

a._____

b._____

c._____

d._____

e._____

Top ten expectations for both spouses:

a. _____

b. _____

c. _____

d. _____

e. _____

f. _____

g. _____

h. _____

i. _____

j. _____

[SESSION SIX]
POWER PLAYS

From Clarence Walker:

"Early in our marriage we had power and control struggles, mainly because we are both strong people. We disagreed over purchases for the home and dealing with our son, among other issues. We had to sit down, talk through our problems, and come to a mutual understanding. She made decisions about home décor while I still gave my input. We divided the decision-making processes concerning our son. We mutually submit to each other based on the pattern of Ephesians 5:1 (submitting yourselves to one another), without taking away from the God-given role of a husband being the head of the home."

Goals for Session Six:
- **To glorify God and bring honor to His name**
- **To enable couples to better understand the role of power and control issues in marital relations**
- **To enable couples to develop the proper amount of power and control**

Lead Couple: Greet couples warmly, begin with opening song, take prayer requests, and lead the couples in an opening prayer.

Prayer Requests:

_____

_____

_____

Lead Couple: Assign Scriptures to couples to read out loud before starting the DVD.

[SESSION SIX]
POWER PLAYS - Cont.

Scripture Reading for Session Six

Genesis 3:16 (NIV)
"To the woman he said, I will greatly increase your pains in childbearing: with pain you will give birth to children. Your desire will be for your husband, and he will rule over you."

Amos 3:3 (NIV)
"Do two walk together unless they have agreed to do so?"

Ephesians 5:21–28 (NIV)
"Submit to one another out of reverence for Christ.

"Wives, submit to your husbands as to the Lord. For the husband is the head of the wife as Christ is the head of the church, his body of which he is the Savior. Now as the church submits to Christ, so also wives should submit to their husbands in everything.

"Husbands, love your wives, just as Christ loved the church and gave himself up for her to make her holy, cleansing her by the washing with water through the word, and to present her to himself as a radiant church, without stain or wrinkle or any other blemish, but hold and blameless. In this same way, husbands ought to love their wives as their own bodies. He who loves his wife loves himself."

Lead Couple: *Play DVD for "Power Plays" and lead a discussion based on the following questions:*

What do you think?

What are some of the decisions that should be made as a couple?

What decisions can you make without your spouse?

If there is a disagreement, who gets the final say?

[SESSION SIX]
POWER PLAYS - Cont.

Sharing Segment

Lead Couple: *"Power and control struggles are common in marriage. They can manifest themselves in disputes about money, child discipline, sex, household duties, etc. Couples must learn to negotiate power and control in the marriage."*

What are the causes of power and control struggles in marriage?

_____

_____

_____

Other examples:
- Women's inherent nature to control versus the man's inherent nature to rule (Genesis 3:16).
- Husbands and wives follow their dominant gender legacies (strong fathers versus strong mothers).
- Feminist philosophies conflict with the chauvinist philosophies.
- Stubborn and proud dispositions
- Insecurity with God-given roles in marriage
- Ignorance of God's plan and roles for husbands and wives

[SESSION SIX]
POWER PLAYS - Cont.

Lead Couple: *"How are these biblical examples of power and control struggles demonstrated in the following Scriptures?"*

Adam and Eve (Genesis 3:11–19)

_____

_____

Job and his wife (Job 2:9–10)

_____

_____

Samson and Delilah (Judges 16:6–17)

_____

_____

How can couples resolve their power and conflict struggles based on Ephesians 5:21–23?

1) Couples submit to _____
   (Ephesians 5:21–23)

   This passage explains how the wife submits and how the husband submits—one by authority and the other by love and sacrifice.

   The Greek word for submitting is *hupo-tasso* (hoop-ot-as-so). *Hupo* means "under" and *tasso* means "to arrange in an orderly fashion"—together, "submitting" means "to arrange in an orderly fashion." The husband and wife must set up order in their home and then get under it.

   It is necessary for each spouse to submit to each other in order to fight together against Satan and his demons according to Ephesians 6:12. With Christ Jesus as their captain (Hebrews 2:10), couples respect each other's positions.

[SESSION SIX]
POWER PLAYS - Cont.

2) Couples must separate authority from power.

After the Fall, God increased man's authority as a balance for the woman's power in Genesis 3:16. The man has a unique position of authority from God to be the head of the home. The woman has the unique position of power to influence the man. If a woman learns properly to use her power of influence, she will not have to usurp his authority.

Authority is the power to determine or settle issues, and power is the ability to do or accomplish something. Power is the ability to influence.

The husband has a right to control with dominion over his home that was delegated to him and backed up by God. The woman has the ability to influence her husband based upon her God-given abilities and skills as a help meet. Her persuasiveness is based upon her greater abilities (all of a woman's senses are stronger than a man).

God delegated His authority to man and it's his job to enforce the rules in the home. The woman gets her power delegated to her by her husband; therefore, she influences the laws of the home as well as her husband.

3) How does Amos 3:3 encourage couples to negotiate and come to agreement about power and authority?

_____

_____

Lead Couple: *Direct the couple's attention to the following exercise and discussion questions.*

Complete the Power/Conflict Struggles Worksheet individually and come together as a couple to share your thoughts. Afterward, discuss as a group the following questions:

- What evidences of power and control struggles do you see in your present relationship?
- What are some of the ways you have tried to deal with the problems?

[SESSION SIX]
POWER PLAYS

Lead Couple: *Read over the home assignment and encourage couples to complete it by the next meeting date.*

Home Assignment:
Complete the Walking in Agreement Worksheet.

Lead Couple: *Close out this session with a song and prayer. Encourage couples to pray together daily. End with a time of refreshments and fellowship.*

[POWER/CONFLICT STRUGGLES WORKSHEET]

1. Do you frequently argue about money, kids, sex, or household responsibilities?

    Yes _____   No _____

2. Do one or both of you need to have the last word in an argument?

    Yes _____   No _____

3. Do you both stubbornly hold on to your position without giving in?

    Yes _____   No _____

4. Do you feel your spouse is the cause of most of your arguments?

    Yes _____   No _____

5. Do you or your spouse complain about feeling crowded, nagged, or controlled?

    Yes _____   No _____

6. Do you feel that you argue a lot with your spouse without resolution?

    Yes _____   No _____

7. Do you or your spouse feel that the other doesn't listen or value their opinions?

    Yes _____   No _____

8. Do you or your spouse complain that the other is uncompromising, stubborn, or likes to always have things their way?

    Yes _____   No _____

9. Do you feel distant from your spouse?

    Yes _____   No _____

10. Have you engaged or have been close to physical fights with your spouse?

    Yes _____   No _____

[POWER/CONFLICT STRUGGLES WORKSHEET]

1. Do you frequently argue about money, kids, sex, or household responsibilities?

   Yes _____   No _____

2. Do one or both of you need to have the last word in an argument?

   Yes _____   No _____

3. Do you both stubbornly hold on to your position without giving in?

   Yes _____   No _____

4. Do you feel your spouse is the cause of most of your arguments?

   Yes _____   No _____

5. Do you or your spouse complain about feeling crowded, nagged, or controlled?

   Yes _____   No _____

6. Do you feel that you argue a lot with your spouse without resolution?

   Yes _____   No _____

7. Do you or your spouse feel that the other doesn't listen or value their opinions?

   Yes _____   No _____

8. Do you or your spouse complain that the other is uncompromising, stubborn, or likes to always have things their way?

   Yes _____   No _____

9. Do you feel distant from your spouse?

   Yes _____   No _____

10. Have you engaged or have been close to physical fights with your spouse?

    Yes _____   No _____

[WALKING IN AGREEMENT WORKSHEET]

1. We agree to submit to each other in the following ways:

HUSBAND SUBMITS BY…	WIFE SUBMITS BY…

2. We agree that the husband is the final authority in the following areas:

a. _____

b. _____

c. _____

d. _____

e. _____

3. We agree that authority is delegated to the wife in the following areas:

a. _____

b. _____

c. _____

d. _____

e. _____

186

[SESSION SEVEN]
IT'S A RELATIVE THING

From Pastor Ja'Ola:

"When Pastor Clarence and I first started dating, his grandmother (who raised him) decided no woman was good enough for her 'Clance Jr.' So she decided she had to break us up. We started praying for her, and I asked the Lord to compass me about with a shield of favor. The Lord turned her heart around, and she loved me and treated me like gold. That was our first success praying together for a family member."

From Clarence Walker;

"My precious mother-in-law was a very strong woman, and she could be intrusive in her own way. She would try to make decisions for us or plan things that involved me, but not ask me. Ja and I discussed the issue, and I asked her to set some boundaries with her mother. I lovingly spoke to my mother-in-law about her intrusiveness, set some boundaries, and reminded her where she overstepped. I eventually became her pastor. She loved and respected me. We had a great relationship."

Goals for Session Seven:
- To glorify God and bring honor to His name
- To help couples better understand the role of in-laws and extended family on marital relations
- To reduce marital conflicts which are caused directly or indirectly by in-laws and other extended relatives

Lead Couple: *Greet couples warmly, begin with opening song, take prayer requests, and lead the couples in an opening prayer*

Prayer Requests:

_____

_____

_____

[SESSION SEVEN]
IT'S A RELATIVE THING - Cont.

Lead Couple: *Assign Scriptures for couples to read out loud before starting the DVD.*

Scripture Reading for Session Seven

Genesis 2:24
"For this reason a man will leave his father and mother and be united to his wife, and they will become one flesh."

Exodus 20:12
"Honor your father and your mother, so that you may live long in the land the Lord your God is giving you."

Matthew 10:34–36
"Do not suppose that I have come to bring peace to the earth. I did not come to bring peace, but a sword. For I have come to turn a man against his father, a daughter against her mother, a daughter-in-law against her mother-in-law—a man's enemies will be the members of his own household."

2 Corinthians 12:14
"Now I am ready to visit you for the third time, and I will not be a burden to you, because what I want is not your possessions but you. After all, children should not have to save up for their parents, but parents for their children."

Lead Couple: *Play DVD for "It's a Relative Thing" and lead a discussion based on the following questions:*

What do you think?

What do you think are the proper roles of extended family in a marital relationship?
Is there certain information that shouldn't be shared with extended family?
Who should resolve any problems with in-laws?

[SESSION SEVEN]
IT'S A RELATIVE THING - Cont.

Sharing Segment

Lead Couple: *"In-laws and extended relatives can be a tremendous source of support or conflict. As a married couple, your first commitment is to each other. Unrestrained in-law involvement can lead to:*

Issues of divided loyalties between spouse and blood relatives
Loss of financial security
In-laws engaged in couple conflicts
In-laws attempting to control or influence a spouse."

The Hebrew word for leave is *azab* (aw-zab) which means "to loosen, relinquish, permit, or forsake." Here are some examples of evidence that a spouse hasn't left the home yet:

- Puts their parents' needs before their spouse's needs
- Allows parents to interfere and become involved in couple's issues
- Involved in parents' problems
- Holds on to some value, philosophy, or system received from parents
- Physically still in parents' home
- Repeating negative behavior patterns of parents
- Parents' influence exceeds spouse's influence

What should a husband or wife do when they realize that they are still cleaving to their parents?

_____

_____

_____

[SESSION SEVEN]
IT'S A RELATIVE THING - Cont.

Suggestions for leaving parental control and cleaving to spouse:

1) Set limits on parental involvement
2) Identify and withstand parental pressures and manipulations
3) Be willing to risk alienation to break bonds
4) Must physically relocate from parents' home
5) Develop a self-identity apart from parents
6) Overcome guilt regarding leaving parents
7) Develop own economic base independent of parents
8) Deal with unfinished issues and develop new relationship with parents

Lead Couple: *"Let's divide up the following Scriptures and learn the positive examples of in-law relations."*

Terah to Sarah (Genesis 11:31)   Jethro to Moses (Exodus 18:1–27)
Naomi to Ruth (Ruth 1:14–18)   Jonathan to David (1 Samuel 18:1–4)
Peter's mother-in-law (Mark 1:29–31, Luke 4:38)

Characteristics of positive in-law interaction:

_____

_____

_____

Lead Couple: *"Negative examples of in-laws are:"*

Lot's sons-in-law (Genesis 19:14)   Judah to Tamar (Genesis 38:24–27)
Saul to David (1 Samuel 18:8–15)   Eli to Phinehas' wife (1 Samuel 4:19–22)
Ahab to Ahaziah (2 Kings 8:26–27)   Annas to Caiphas (John 18:12–14)

Characteristics of negative in-law interaction:

_____

_____

_____

There are seven steps for dealing with in-laws:

1) Set boundaries on their involvement with your marriage. What kind of boundaries should be set?

_____

_____

2) Put your marriage partner before all in-laws. What are some ways that you can do this?

_____

_____

3) Accept their wisdom, and make use of their life experiences when you ask for it. What are some life experiences that you as a couple could glean from your in-laws?

_____

_____

4) Visit at least one family event to get a feel of your spouse's family. What family events could you attend as a couple?

_____

_____

5) Accept the fact that your Christian faith will naturally create division with unsaved relatives. Why do you think that being a believer will cause issues with in-laws?

_____

_____

6) Give your in-laws honor and respect whether you feel they deserve it or not. Why should you treat them with honor and respect?

_____

_____

7) Be assertive when necessary but avoid intense, open conflict. What are some ways that couples can resist being pulled into harsh arguments?

_____

_____

[SESSION SEVEN]
IT'S A RELATIVE THING - Cont.

Lead Couple: *Read over home assignment and encourage couples to complete it by the next meeting date.*

Home Assignment:

Review over the boundaries for dealing with in-laws, and incorporate them into your relationships with in-laws over the next week.

Lead Couple: *Close out the session with a song and prayer. Encourage couples to pray together daily. End with a time of refreshments and fellowship.*

[SESSION EIGHT]
TIME TO CHILL

From the Walkers:

"With our ministry, church, and family responsibilities, making time for our relationship was no longer an option—it became survival. We take four vacations a year with three of those just for us as a couple. Even when money is tight, we turn the phones off, put a stop on the mail, go to the movies, take day trips and pretend we are out of town. If we miss a getaway, we tend to get irritable and snappy with each other. Even Jesus had to pull away from ministry and spend time alone."

Goals for Session Eight:
- **To glorify God and bring honor to His name**
- **To help couples better understand the importance of time management in relationship to marriage**
- **To enable them to find more leisure time for themselves as individuals as well as a couple**

Lead Couple: *Greet couples warmly, begin with opening song, take prayer requests, and lead the couples in an opening prayer.*

Prayer Requests:

_____

_____

_____

Lead Couple: *Assign Scriptures to couples to read out loud before starting the DVD.*

[SESSION EIGHT]
TIME TO CHILL - Cont.

Scripture Reading for Session Eight

Deuteronomy 24:5
"If a man has recently married, he must not set to war or have any duty laid on him. For one year he is to be free to stay at home and bring happiness to the wife he has married."

Ecclesiastes 9:9
"Enjoy life with your wife, whom you love, all the days of this meaningless life that God has given you under the sun—all your meaningless days."

Song of Solomon 5:2–3
"I slept but my heart was awake. Listen! My lover is knocking: 'Open to me, my sister, my darling, my dove, my flawless one. My head is drenched with dew, my hair with the dampness of the night.'

"I have taken off my robe—must I put it on again? I have washed my feet—must I soil them again?"

John 4:6
"Jacob's well was there, and Jesus, tired as he was from the journey, sat down by the well."

Lead Couple: *Play DVD for "A Time to Chill" and lead a discussion based on the following questions:*

What do you think?

How do you balance kids, career, and ministry?
What order should each come in?
What happens if your priorities aren't in the right order?

[SESSION EIGHT]
TIME TO CHILL - Cont.

Sharing Segment

Lead Couple: *"In this high-speed, overly scheduled, and stressful society, finding leisure time is difficult. However, couples must make time for each other in order for their marriage to thrive."*

What do the following teach us about the significance of our leisure?

Deuteronomy 24:5 _____

_____

Exodus 31:15–17 _____

_____

Ephesians 5:15–16 _____

_____

Ecclesiastes 9:9 _____

_____

John 4:6 _____

_____

[SESSION EIGHT]
TIME TO CHILL - Cont.

How has the lack of leisure time affected your marriage?

_____

_____

_____

Has leisure time ever positively affected your marriage? How?

_____

_____

Lead Couple: *"Leisure is the freedom from work or consuming duties. God made the heaven and earth in six days and rested on the seventh. He has that same expectation for believers today—that they would take out time to rest. There are five ways in which leisure can enhance your marriage."*

1) Leisure relieves stress which can be a major cause of conflict in marriage.

2) Leisure enhances intimacy by providing time for couples to spend together.

3) Leisure improves the physical health of couples.

4) Leisure enhances positive communication.

5) Leisure enables couples to be more well-rounded.

How can your marriage benefit from one or more of the above?

_____

_____

_____

[SESSION EIGHT]
TIME TO CHILL - Cont.

Lead Couple: *"Circle all that apply that reflects how you as a couple can get more out of your leisure time."*

a.) Take a vacation
b.) Create a day of Sabbath when no work is done
c.) Get involved with a hobby (preferably stress-reducing hobbies)
d.) Participate in family games and recreation
e.) Re-evaluate your time schedule to see how you can increase your leisure time
f.) Avoid taking on more work and overtime
g.) Follow the example of Jesus Christ (He sat by the well when He was weary)
h.) Pay attention to the body's signals of needing more rest
i.) Abandon workaholic philosophies which devalue leisure time

Any more ideas?

j. _____

k. _____

l. _____

Lead Couple: *Read over home assignment and encourage couples to complete it by the next meeting date.*

Home Assignment:

Complete the Work Time Assessment and Leisure Time Evaluation Forms.

Lead Couple: *Close out this session with a song and prayer. Encourage couples to pray together daily. End with a time of refreshments and fellowship.*

[WORK TIME ASSESSMENT FORM]

ACTIVITY	TIME PER MONTH / WEEK / DAY	SAME	INCREASE YOUR TIME (+)	DECREASE YOUR TIME (-)
Primary job				
Secondary job				
Overtime work				
Community involvement				
Ministry Commitments				
- Choir				
- Deacon				
- Greeters				
- Prison ministry				
- Sunday School				
- Music ministry				
- Youth ministry				
- Marriage ministry				
- Coaching				

[LEISURE TIME EVALUATION FORM]

ACTIVITY	TIME PER MONTH / WEEK / DAY	SAME	INCREASE (+)	DECREASE (-)
Sleeping				
Exercise				
Reading				
Watching TV				
Gardening				
Eating out				
Listening to music				
Visiting friends				
Theater				
Cooking				

200

[SESSION NINE]
WORKING PEOPLE

From Pastor Clarence:

"As a Marriage and Family Therapist, I decided that I would not bring people's troubles home with me. I set boundaries for my clients: they couldn't call me at home, and they had a process to follow for emergencies. I worked a lot of evenings and often came home late. My wife and I discussed my schedule; we needed to be in agreement, and if I was running late, I would call her. We made it a point to schedule couple and family time in addition to my work schedule."

Goals for Session Nine:
- To glorify God and bring honor to His name
- To help couples better understand the ethic of employment, vocation, and education on marital relations
- To enable couples to reduce the negative effects of work on the their marriage

Lead Couple: *Greet couples warmly, begin with opening song, take prayer requests, and lead the couples in an opening prayer.*

Prayer Requests:

_____

_____

_____

Lead Couple: *Assign Scriptures to couples to read out loud before starting the DVD.*

[SESSION NINE]
WORKING PEOPLE - Cont.

Scripture Reading for Session Nine

Genesis 2:15
"The Lord God took the man and put him in the Garden of Eden to work it and take care of it."

Genesis 3:19
"By the sweat of your brow you will eat your food until you return to the ground, since from it you were taken; for dust you are and to dust you will return."

Proverbs 24:27
"Finish your outdoor work and get your field ready; after that, build your house."

Proverbs 31:17
"She sets about her work vigorously; her arms are strong for her tasks."

Lead Couple: *Play DVD for "Working People" and lead a discussion based on the following questions.*

What do you think?

How can a spouse's job affect the relationship?
Can you think of a situation where employment affected your marriage?
How did you handle it?
What does Scripture teach couples about balancing work and marriage?

Sharing Segment

Lead Couple: *"Work is important for the support and continuation of the family, but if there is not an understanding and some communicated boundaries, it can cause problems."*

[SESSION NINE]
WORKING PEOPLE - Cont.

Lead Couple: *Conflict in marriage due to employment can take on many forms:*

- Frustration with the job can spill over into the marriage.
- Dual career couples can have power and control struggles.
- Work can take away from valuable family time.
- Job changes or losses can create stress on the marriage.

How can any of the above cause conflict in a marriage?

_____

_____

_____

Lead Couple: *"What does the Bible teach about work?"*

1) Work requires balance in marriage.
   What do you learn about Adam's work in Genesis 3:17?

   _____

   _____

   _____

   _____

[SESSION NINE]
WORKING PEOPLE - Cont.

2) Work is a prerequisite before marriage.
   When did God put Adam to work in Genesis 2:15, before or after Eve?

   _____

   Why do you think God did it in that order?

   _____
   _____

3) Work is an indicator of marital love.
   How did Jacob prove his love for Rachael in Genesis 29:18, 25–27?

   _____
   _____

4) Work shouldn't take priority over the health and well-being of a family.
   How do 3 John 2 and Proverbs 17:1 support the statement above?

   _____
   _____

5) Work is necessary. What do 2 Thessalonians 3:10 and 1 Timothy 5:8 reveal about my work and family?

   _____
   _____

[SESSION NINE]
WORKING PEOPLE - Cont.

What are some options for couples who are feeling stressed about their jobs?

1. Pursue another career.

2. Work toward one spouse staying home.

3. Become an entrepreneur of your skill and be self-employed.

4. _____

5. _____

Lead Couple: "It is becoming more uncommon for one spouse to be able to stay at home, while the other goes to work. In Proverbs 31, we find a woman who was able to not only stay home, but also bring in significant income to support her family. She had multiple roles:

- as a wife (vv. 11, 23, and 28)
- as a mother (v. 28)
- as a working woman (v. 24)
- as a community server (v. 20)

"Is this still possible today? Why or why not?"

_____

_____

Lead Couple: *Read the following exercise for the couples to do and answer the discussion questions as a group.*

Each couple needs to think of five words that describe the impact of their employment on their marriage and individually write them on a sheet of paper. Couples should exchange notes, review the list, and express their interpretation of what each spouse is trying to communicate.

It's important for each spouse to take turns in receiving and interpreting without defenses or judgment. Spouses should be invited to correct, clarify, or elaborate on their interpretation.

What challenges has your job brought to your marriage?

[SESSION NINE]
WORKING PEOPLE - Cont.

What benefit has your employment brought to your marriage?

Do you need to make any adjustments? If so, what?

Lead Couple: *Read over home assignment and encourage couples to complete it by the next meeting date.*

Home Assignment

Complete the Couple Work Assignment Assessment sheet.

Lead Couple: *Close out this session with a song and prayer. Encourage couples to pray together daily. End with a time of refreshments and fellowship.*

[Couple Work Assignment Assessment]

1. Elements of work we are pleased with:

    a. _____

    b. _____

    c. _____

    d. _____

    e. _____

2. Elements of work we want to see changed or improved:

    a. _____

    b. _____

    c. _____

    d. _____

    e. _____

3. Things we will commit to change or improve:

    a. _____

    b. _____

    c. _____

    d. _____

    e. _____

    f. _____

    g. _____

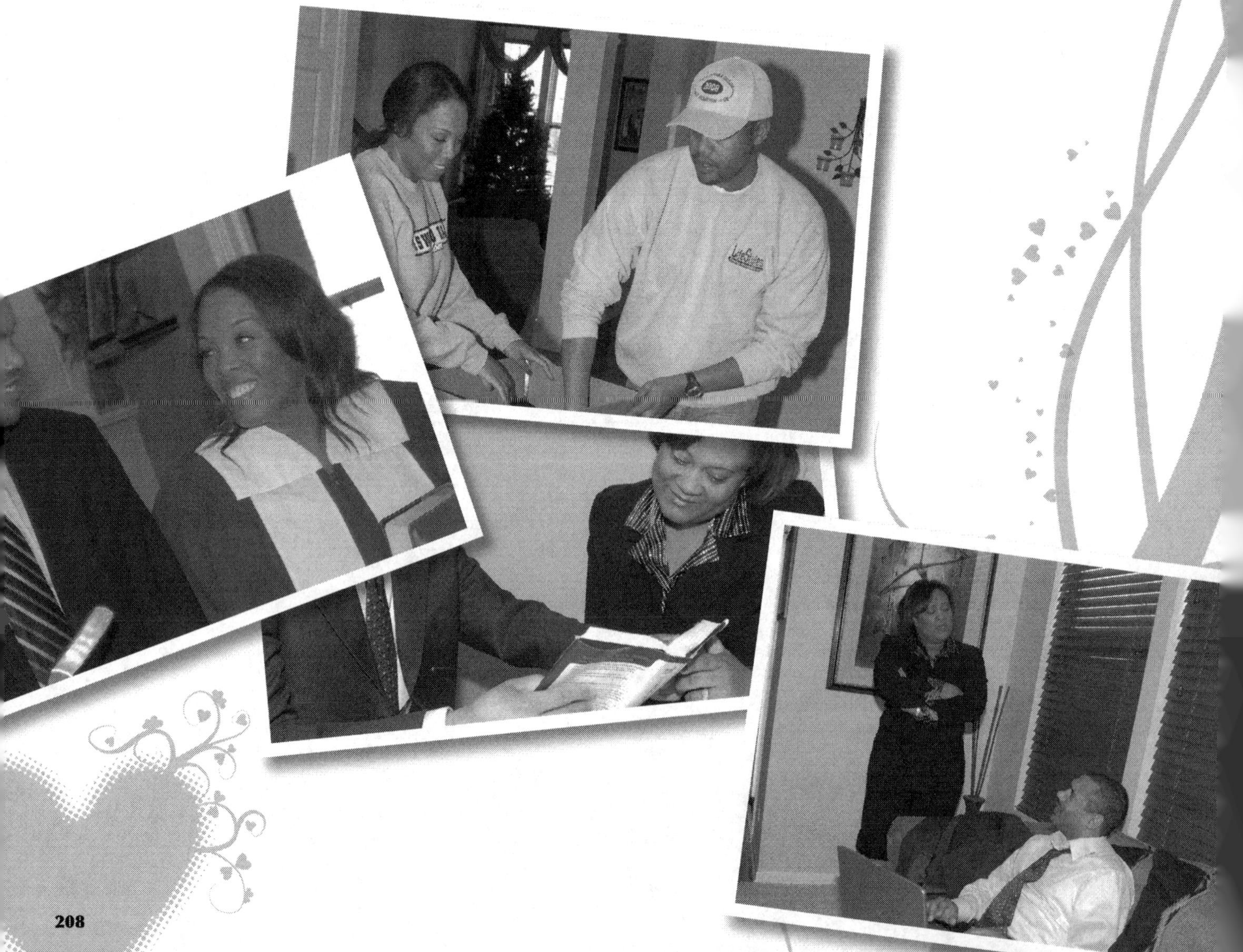

[SESSION TEN]
HAVING CHURCH

From the Walkers:

"We traveled a lot in ministering to other churches, yet until we became pastors, we never realized the incredible difference of having a loving church to support our marriage and family. Our church family encouraged us through the deaths of three parents in four months' time. Church ministry is necessary for spiritual growth for our marriage. Yet we've learned to balance family and ministry which oftentimes means that we needed to set boundaries to protect our marriage, family, and church."

Goals for Session Ten:
- **To glorify God and bring honor to His name**
- **To help couples understand the importance of church activities and ministry on marriage**
- **To enable couples to balance ministry responsibilities in their marriage**

Lead Couple: *Greet couples warmly, begin with opening song, take prayer requests, and lead the couples in an opening prayer.*

Prayer Requests:

_____

_____

_____

Lead Couple: *Assign Scriptures to couples to read aloud before starting the DVD.*

[SESSION TEN]
HAVING CHURCH - Cont.

Scripture Reading for Session Ten

Joshua 24:15
"But as for me and my household, we will serve the Lord."

Acts 2:42–47
"They devoted themselves to the apostles' teaching and to the fellowship, to the breaking of bread and to prayer. Everyone was filled with awe, and many wonders and miraculous signs were done by the apostles. All the believers were together and had everything in common. Selling their possessions and goods, they gave to anyone as he had need. Every day they continued to meet together in the temple courts. They broke bread in their homes and ate together with glad and sincere hearts, praising God and enjoying the favor of all the people. And the Lord added to their number daily those who were being saved."

Hebrews 10:25
"Let us not give up meeting together, as some are in the habit of doing, but let use encourage one another—and all the more as you see the Day approaching."

Lead Couple: *Play the DVD for "Having Church" and lead the discussion based on the following questions:*

What do you think?

How do you prioritize in your household?

How can couples balance ministry responsibilities with marriage and family obligations?

[SESSION TEN]
HAVING CHURCH - Cont.

Sharing Segment

Lead Couple: *"Ministry responsibilities are an important part of the Christian walk; however, conflicts concerning the church can create volatility in the marriage."*

Why is the church important to the marriage and family? Look up the Scriptures after each statement that demonstrates the value of church to the family.

1. Couples gain knowledge of God's plan for their marriage and family through sound teaching in the church.

Titus 2:2–8 _____

_____

Ephesians 5:21–30 _____

_____

_____

2. Church provides a community support system for married couples and families.

Hebrews 10:25 _____

_____

3. Church provides an accountability system for the behavior of husbands and wives.

Acts 2:41–43 _____

_____

Acts 5:1–18 _____

_____

[SESSION TEN]
HAVING CHURCH - Cont.

4. Church provides an opportunity for couples and families to serve the body of Christ.

Hebrews 10:25 _____

_____

Romans 12:11 _____

_____

5. Church provides positive role models for each member of the family.

1 Timothy 4:12 _____

_____

2 Thessalonians 3:7 _____

_____

Lead Couple: *If there isn't balance between family and ministry responsibilities, many conflicts can arise in the marriage including:*

- One spouse who spends too much time at the church while neglecting the marriage and family
- Conflicts over theological differences
- Differences in levels of spiritual growth
- Power and control struggles over one spouse's leadership and recognition in the church
- Jealous feelings are aroused if one spouse works closely with someone of the opposite sex
- Couples taking different sides in a church dispute
- Disagreements over how much money to give over to the church

[SESSION TEN]
HAVING CHURCH - Cont.

What are some ways that couples can overcome the conflicts above for their marriage?

For example, couples can set boundaries on the amount of time they will put into ministry and make sure they have also invested into marriage and family.

_____

_____

_____

Lead Couple: *"How has your church involvement positively affected your marriage?"*

_____

_____

_____

_____

_____

Lead Couple: *Read over the home assignment and encourage couples to complete it by the next meeting date.*

Home Assignment:

On separate sheets of paper each spouse should make a list of how their marriage has positively impacted the church. Each partner should take turns sharing each item on the list with each other. Afterward, discuss any changes that you as a couple can make to keep the balance between marriage, family, and ministry.

Lead Couple: *Close out this session with a song and prayer. Encourage couples to pray together daily. End with a time of refreshments and fellowship.*

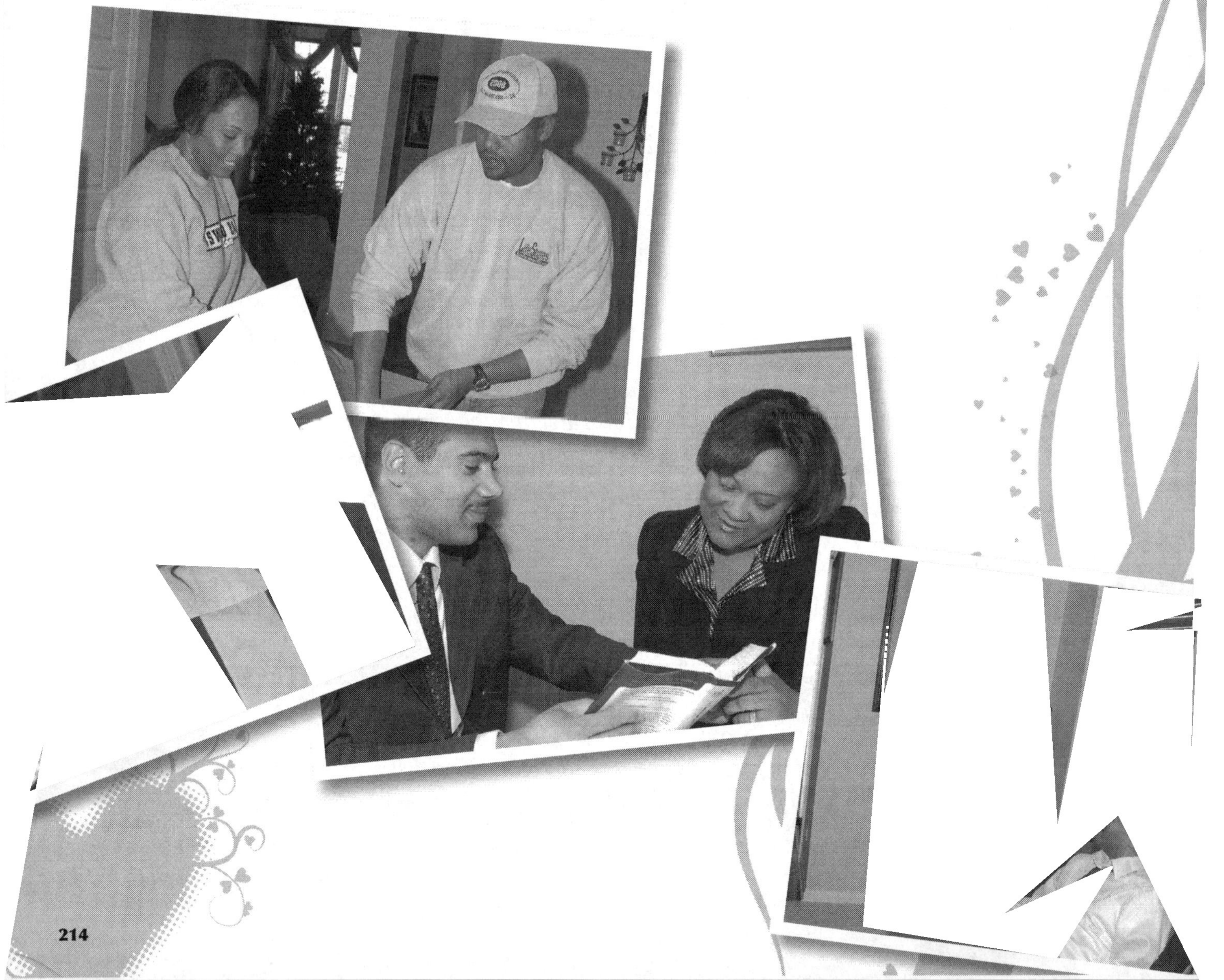

[SESSION ELEVEN]
TO MOVE OR NOT TO MOVE

From the Walkers:
"When we built a new home, we had to fight to get a mortgage. The bank took us through the wringer, but we walked in the authority of the Lord. We prayed and it was approved. Moving was a stressful process, but it can be the beginning of new hopes and dreams when we sought direction from the Lord."

Goals for Session Eleven:
- **To glorify God and bring honor to His name**
- **To help couples understand the impact on their marriage of issues related to residence and moving**
- **To enable couples to reduce the negative effects of moving on their marriage**

Lead Couple: *Greet couples warmly, begin with opening song, take prayer requests, and lead the couples in an opening prayer.*

Prayer Requests:

_____

_____

_____

Lead Couple: *Assign Scriptures to couples to read out loud before starting the DVD.*

[SESSION ELEVEN]
TO MOVE OR NOT TO MOVE - Cont.

Scripture Reading for Session Eleven

Genesis 2:24
"For this reason a man will leave his father and mother and be united to this wife, and they will become one flesh."

Exodus 33:1–2
"Then the Lord said to Moses, 'Leave this place, you and the people you brought up out of Egypt, and go up to the land I promised on oath to Abraham, Isaac, and Jacob, saying, 'I will give it to your descendants.'"

Matthew 10:11–13
"Whatever town or village you enter, search for some worthy person there and stay at his house until you leave. As you enter the home, give it your greeting. If the home is deserving, let your peace rest on it; if it is not, let your peace return to you."

Lead Couple: *Play DVD for "To Move or Not to Move" and lead a discussion based on the following questions:*

What do you think?

What should couples consider before moving?
What are the positive and negative implications of moving on a marriage?

Sharing Segment

Lead Couple: *"Decisions concerning moving can cause tension and conflict in a marriage. Couples need to deal with this issue from a biblical perspective."*

[SESSION ELEVEN]
TO MOVE OR NOT TO MOVE - Cont.

What are the reasons for moving in the following biblical examples?

1) Genesis 2:24 _____

_____

2) Genesis 12:1, 18; Genesis 31:3, 35:1, 46:2–3 _____

_____

3) Genesis 19:12–22 _____

_____

4) Exodus 33:1–2 _____

_____

5) Ruth 1:6–15 _____

_____

6) Matthew 2:13–14 _____

_____

7) Genesis 46:5–7 _____

_____

8) Genesis 27:43–44 _____

_____

9) 2 Kings 4:8–17 _____

_____

[SESSION ELEVEN]
TO MOVE OR NOT TO MOVE - Cont.

Lead Couple: *"How do the following examples reflect poor decision making in their moving?"*

a. Eviction (Genesis 3:22–24) _____

_____

b. Running from God (Jonah 1:1–17) _____

_____

c. Quest for materialism and property (Genesis 13:10–13) _____

_____

d. Family dispute (Genesis 31:1–3, 22–31) _____

_____

Lead Couple: *Instruct the couples to do the following exercise:*

Think of a time when you and your family had to move. With a separate sheet of paper, each spouse should list the challenges this presented to your marriage. Afterward, have a group discussion using the following questions and the list:

What were the specific challenges to the marriage?
How did you as a couple cope with the challenges?
Were any of the biblical reasons for moving reflected?
What lessons did you learn for any future moves?

Lead Couple: *Read over home assignment and encourage couples to complete it by the next meeting date.*

Home Assignment:

Complete the Moving Boundaries worksheet

Lead Couple: *Close out this session with a song and prayer. Encourage couples to pray together daily. End with a time of refreshments and fellowship.*

[MOVING GUIDELINES WORKSHEET]

Make a chronological list of things you will need to do in the event that your family needs to make a decision about moving. You can use tips at the bottom of the page in addition to your own ideas.

Things we will do in making a moving decision:

1) _____
2) _____
3) _____
4) _____
5) _____
6) _____
7) _____
8) _____
9) _____
10) _____

Tips in Moving

Following the Lord's leading

Be persistent and determined

Develop and implement stress-reducing activities

Anticipate setbacks

Be organized

Plan early

Make family prayer a priority

Be methodical and systematic

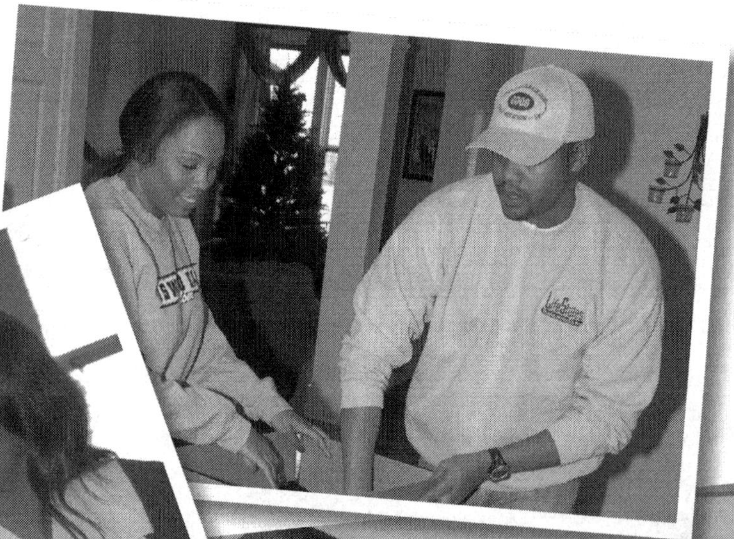

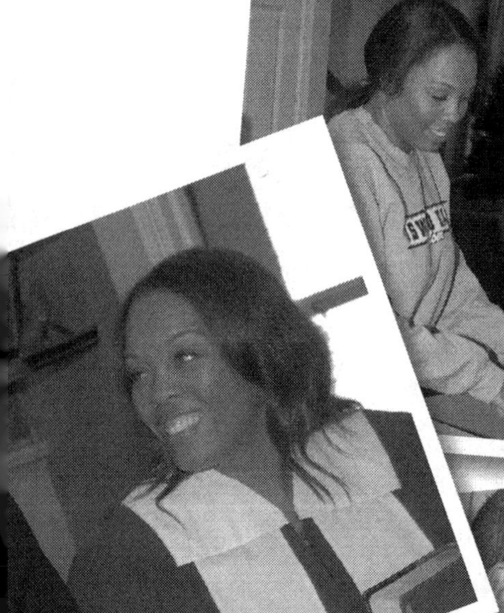

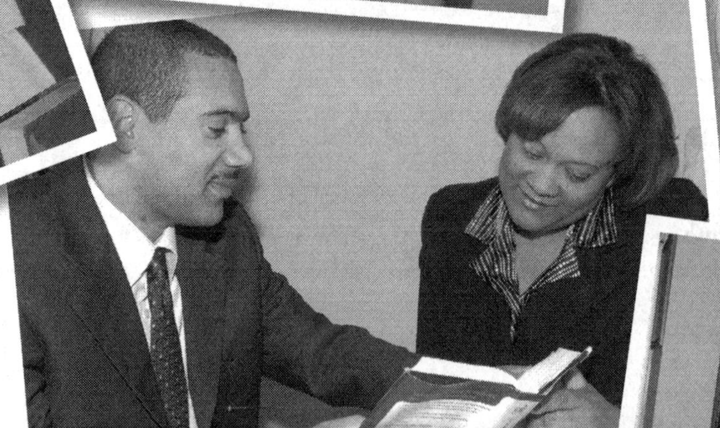

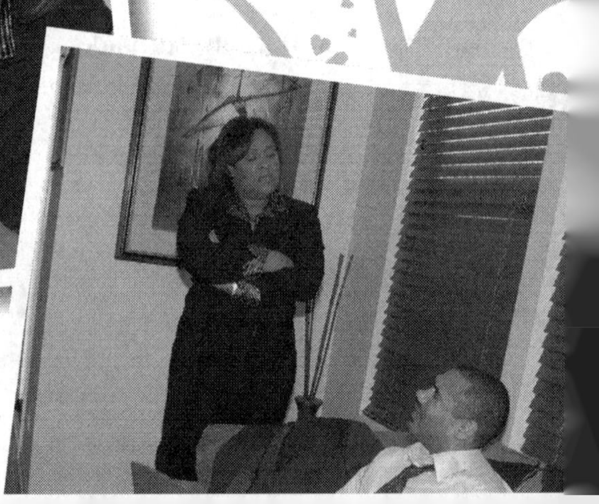

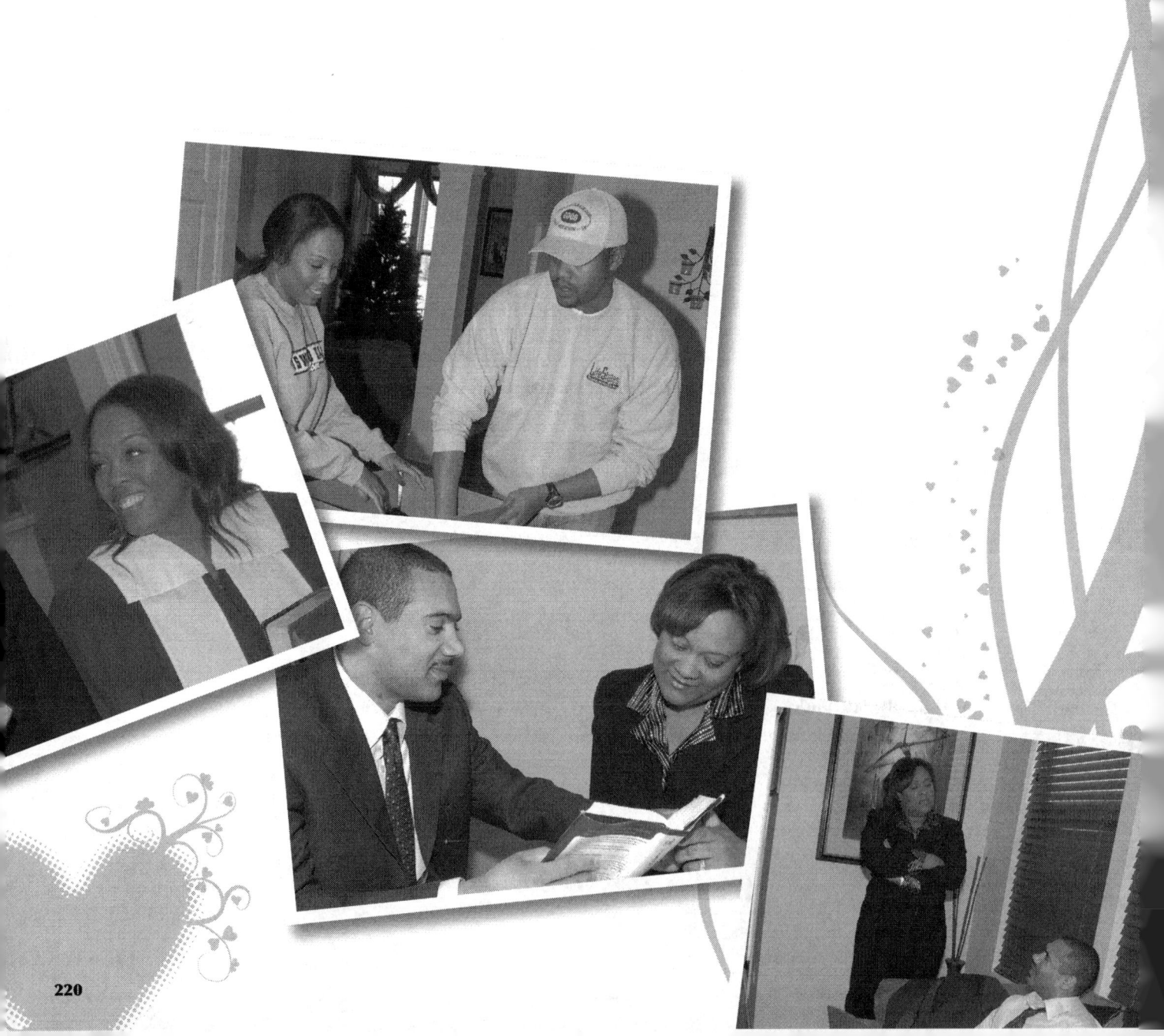

[SESSION TWELVE]
OUR COVENANT OF LOVE

From Pastor Ja'Ola:

"My parents went home to be with the Lord after sixty-three years of marriage. What made them stick together? They never lost the desire to keep growing. They kept a teachable spirit even when they were both in their nineties. When your love gets tired and starts to dry up, just pull up to God's filling station of agape love. Ask Him to supernaturally love your spouse through you. He will renew your love both for friendship and romance as well as establish your hearts to love each other unconditionally. So when your honey steps into a room, your heart will still skip a beat. My heart does, and I say to myself, 'There's my baby, and I'm in love all over again.'"

Goals for Session Twelve:
- **To glorify God and bring honor to His name**
- **To help couples gain an appreciation for the seriousness of a covenant as it relates to marriage**
- **To prepare them for the covenant ceremony and communion**

Lead Couple: *Greet couples warmly, begin with opening song, take prayer requests, and lead the couples in an opening prayer.*

Prayer Requests:

_____

_____

_____

Lead Couple: *Assign Scriptures to couples to read out loud before starting the DVD.*

[SESSION TWELVE]
OUR COVENANT OF LOVE - Cont.

Scripture Reading for Session Twelve

Malachi 2:13–14
"Another thing you do: You flood the Lord's altar with tears. You weep and wail because he no longer pays attention to your offerings or accepts them with pleasure from your hands. You ask, 'Why?' It is because the Lord is acting as the witness between you and the wife of your youth, because you have broken faith with her, though she is your partner, the wife of your marriage covenant."

Proverbs 2:16–17
"It will save you also from the adulteress, from the wayward wife with her seductive words, who has left the partner of her youth and ignored the covenant she made before God."

2 Corinthians 3:6
"He has made us competent as ministers of a new covenant—not of the letter but of the Spirit; for the letter kills, but the Spirit gives life."

Lead Couple: *Play DVD for "Our Covenant of Love" and lead a discussion based on the following questions:*

What do you think?

What are some strategies you can incorporate to protect your marriage?
What work needs to be done to keep your marriage strong?
What does the Bible teach about marriage?

Sharing Segment

Lead Couple: *"We see how serious the Lord takes the marriage covenant by the words directly from Jesus on the subject."*

Matthew 19:4-6—"'Haven't you read', he replied, 'that at the beginning the Creator made them male and female, and said "For this reason a man will leave his father and mother and be united to his wife and the two will become one flesh"? So they are no longer two, but one. Therefore what God has joined together, let man not separate.'"

Matthew 19:8—"Jesus replied, 'Moses permitted you to divorce your wives because your hearts were hard. But it was not this way from the beginning, I tell you that anyone who divorces his wife, except for marital unfaithfulness, and marries another woman commits adultery.'"

[SESSION TWELVE]
OUR COVENANT OF LOVE - Cont.

Lead Couple: *"A covenant is a treaty, confederacy, or pledge. Why is covenant so important to God based on the following Scriptures?"*

Malachi 2:13–14 _____

_____

1 Chronicles 16:15, 17 _____

_____

The Lord was and is always serious about His covenants, and wants every married couple to be as well. He remembers His covenant forever—the word He commanded for a thousand generations—the covenant He made with Abraham, the oath He swore to Jacob, and He confirmed it to Jacob as a decree to Israel as an everlasting covenant.

What are the advantages of having a marriage covenant?

- Spells out the terms of the agreement clearly and specifically

- Involves God as a Witness and Enforcer

- Encourages couples to be committed to the relationship no matter what

- Helps couples appreciate the seriousness of the marital relationship

- Engages couples toward conflict resolution

- Causes couples to rely on God's power to stick it out

- Provides a standard of measuring marital success and growth

- Allows for an accountability structure

Which of these advantages of having a covenant has benefited your marriage the most?

_____

_____

223

[SESSION TWELVE]
OUR COVENANT OF LOVE - Cont.

What are some consequences of breaking your marriage covenant?

_____

_____

_____

_____

Lead Couple: *"The following is the process of making a covenant. Why is each part necessary for the covenant of marriage?"*

1) Identification—each partner identifies all their expectations

Why is this necessary? _____

_____

2) Communication—each partner shares these expectations with each other

Why is this necessary? _____

_____

3) Negotiation—couples negotiate each expectation

Why is this necessary? _____

_____

4) Documentation—couples write out expectations on a form

Why is this necessary? _____

_____

[SESSION TWELVE]
OUR COVENANT OF LOVE - Cont.

5) Sanctification—ceremony is carried out to formalize and sanction

Why is this necessary? _____

_____

6) Application—covenant is put into practice on a daily basis

Why is this necessary? _____

_____

7) Evaluation—couples sit down at least once a week to evaluate the covenant

Why is this necessary? _____

_____

Lead Couple: *Instruct each couple to pull out the FCLO covenant in their books and have them ready to repeat after you.*

[FCLO Covenant]

Husband: I covenant before the Lord to pray daily for my family and keep a pure heart before the Lord. I will ask Him to fill me with His Spirit, and to empower me to love my wife as He loves the Church. I will choose to forgive and by God's grace protect her, cherish her and meet her needs. I will fill my home with His Word and His peace by loving God first, myself, and then honoring and regarding my wife.

Wife: I covenant to the Lord and pray for my family on a daily basis. I will ask the Lord to fill me with His love and empower me to respect my husband. I will use the words of my mouth to bring life and healing to my family. I will fill my home with His Word and His peace by loving God first, then myself, and then honoring and regarding my husband.

Husband and Wife: (facing each other while holding hands)

As we journey through this life together we covenant to put the Lord first in our home. We will pray together and make time to speak life and build each other up. We will put on the armor of God and resist all attacks on our love, and by His grace and power we will be examples to the world of God's love for His Church.

Lead Couple: *Close with a song and prayer. Encourage couples to pray together daily. End this final session with a time of refreshments and fellowship.*

[Reference:]

Strong, James. *The Exhaustive Concordance of the Bible*: Electronic edition. Ontario: Woodside Bible Fellowship, 1996.

227

The Walkers have a full line of training for a successful marriage, family and single life that can be ordered from UMI's website – www.urbanministries.com.

Visit www.urbanministries.com for the following resources and many others:

Crazy Communication
There are certain crazy patterns of communication that we all fall into. Dr Walker teaches Bible methods of effective communication in marriage and single relationships.
1 CD $12.00

So, What Do You Want From Me?
An essential message concerning what it takes to keep your mate content in marriage.
2 CDs $15.00

Honorable Marriage - Original Music CD
Honorable marriage is the way that we're styled, the Lord said that our bed is undefiled.
CD $8.00

Honorable Marriage - Edu-Music Series
This is a combination of teaching and music on Biblical sexual intimacy. Sex was God's idea.
2 CDs $20.00

Biblical Parenting 101
Powerful, practical, Biblical basic training for every parent.
2 CDs $15.00

Blended and Blessed
How to overcome step family problems.
Biblical, practical ways to blend families.
CD $12.00

Bone of my Bone
God is the one who made male and female different. Learn to appreciate and understand His purpose for each. Viva la difference!
2 CD $15.00

Breaking Generational Family Problems
Identify the family scripts, roles and legacies that keep us in bondage from one generation to the next. God has a plan for your deliverance. Powerful, practical teaching by the Walkers.
2 CDs $15.00

Can We Talk?
Resolving conflicts and negotiating issues is key to a successful marriage and family—learn how.
CD $12.00

Coping With the Unsaved Mate
Dr. Walker discusses the three types of unbelieving partners and how to deal with each.
2 CDs $15.00

Dare to Reconcile
Dr. C. Walker shares on the powerful concept of confession and forgiveness, the keys to unlock your heart from the prison of pain. For all relationships.
2 CDs $15.00

Healing the Hurts of the Home
Learn the cause, the characteristics and the cure for marital hurts.
1 CDs $12.00

Help Lord, There's A Teenager in the House
Help to understand and know how to deal with your teenager. Dr. C. Walker even shares the names of the demonic spirits that attack your teens.
3 CD $19.00

How to Devil Proof Your Marriage
Dr. Clarence teaches Christian couples the warfare they will need to wage to protect their marriage from the attacks of Satan. Don't be defenseless, learn to fight together.
2 CD $15.00

In Laws, Out Laws and God's Laws
An inspiring message on how to change negative relationships with your in-laws.
1 CDs $12.00

Whose Side Are You On?
This exciting teaching by Dr. Ja and Dr. Clarence deals with the six sides of the man and woman. We each must learn to deal with the little girl, the king, the warrior, the mother, etc. in our spouse. Ladies, if you don't deal properly with the king in your husband you will soon be dealing with his warrior. Brothers, if you don't properly set boundaries for the mother side of your wife you will have power and control struggles. This is a fun, but powerful training that is helpful in all male/female relationships but is especially crucial for husbands and wives. It is based on the life examples in the Word of God that is our answer for all things.
3 CD's $19.00

[Notes]

[Notes]

[Notes]

[Notes]

[Notes]

[Notes]